THE NEW
THEOLOGIAN

Other books by Ved Mehta

FACE TO FACE

WALKING THE INDIAN STREETS

FLY AND THE FLY-BOTTLE

THE NEW
THEOLOGIAN

VED MEHTA

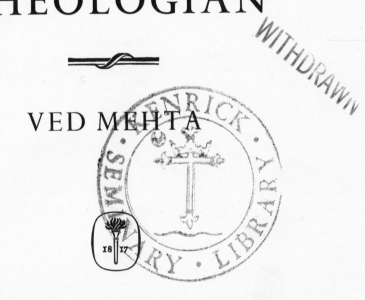

HARPER & ROW, PUBLISHERS

NEW YORK, EVANSTON, AND LONDON

Permission is acknowledged for excerpts on pp. 8, 9, and 10 from *Honest to God* by John A. T. Robinson. © 1963, SCM Press Ltd., London. Published U.S.A., 1963, The Westminster Press.

Permission is acknowledged for excerpts on pp. 26, 27, 28, 29, 30, 31, 54, and 55 from *The Honest to God Debate,* edited by David L. Edwards and John A. T. Robinson. © 1963, SCM Press Ltd., London. Published U.S.A., 1963, The Westminster Press.

Permission is acknowledged for the quotation on pp. 21 and 22 from "Historical Objections" by A. R. Vidler, © 1963 by A. R. Vidler, from *Objections to Christian Belief,* published by J. B. Lippincott Company, Philadelphia, and Constable Publishers, London.

Extracts from letters of Dietrich Bonhoeffer are reprinted by permission of The Macmillan Company from *Prisoner for God: Letters and Papers from Prison* by Dietrich Bonhoeffer, edited by Eberhard Bethge. © 1953 by The Macmillan Company. Permission is also acknowledged from SCM Press Ltd., London.

To the office

CONTENTS

THE NEW
THEOLOGIAN

I

ECCE HOMO

"OUR IMAGE OF GOD MUST GO" was the startling headline on an article by the Right Reverend John Robinson, Suffragan Bishop of Woolwich, that appeared in the London *Observer* for March 17, 1963. An explanation just a little less startling followed: "'Honest to God,' by the Bishop of Woolwich, will be published on Tuesday. In this article the Bishop expresses the main theme of this controversial book: the urgent need to question the traditional image of God as a supernatural Person if Christianity is to survive." "Image" was an advertising word. What did it have to do with God? "Honest to God" was a blasphemy. What was the Bishop doing blaspheming in public? And how, exactly, had a book become "controversial" before it was published? My hackles were up, and the Bishop's article did little to pacify me. "Few people realise that we are in the middle of one of the most exciting theological ferments of the century," it began spectacularly:

New ideas about God and religion, many of them with disturbing revolutionary implications, are breaking surface. If Christianity is to survive it must be relevant to modern secular man, not just to the dwindling number of the religious. . . . Men can no longer credit the existence of "gods" or of a God as a supernatural Person, such as religion has always posited. Not infrequently, as I watch or listen to a broadcast discussion between a Christian and a humanist, I catch myself realising that most of my sympathies are on the humanist's side. . . . The new ideas were first put on record by a German pastor in a Nazi prison in 1944: "Our whole 1,900-year-old Christian preaching and theology rests upon the 'religious premise' of man. . . . If one day it becomes apparent that this *a priori* 'premise' simply does not exist but was an historical and temporary form of human self-expression, *i.e.*, if we reach the stage of being radically without religion—and I think this is more or less the case already—what does that mean for 'Christianity'? *It means that the linchpin is removed from the whole structure of our Christianity to date.*" [The Bishop of Woolwich's italics.]

After noting that these historic words about what the Bishop identified as "religionless Christianity" had been written on April 30, 1944, by Dietrich Bonhoeffer, the imprisoned German pastor, who was executed by the Nazis not long afterward and whose book "Letters and Papers from Prison" was posthumously edited and published by Pastor Eberhard Bethge, a close friend, the article went on:

When his letters were first published—a bare ten years ago—one felt at once that the Church was not ready for what Bonhoeffer was saying. Indeed, it might properly be understood only 100 years hence. But it seemed one of those trickles that must one day split rocks. . . . Modern man has opted for a secular world: he has become increasingly non-religious. The Churches have deplored this as the great defection from God, and the more they write it off, the more this movement has seen itself as anti-Christian. But, claims Bonhoeffer boldly, the period of religion is over. Man is growing out of it: he is "coming of age." By that he doesn't mean that he is getting better (a prisoner of the Gestapo had few illusions about human nature) but that for good or for ill he is putting the religious world-view behind him as childish and pre-scientific.

All this was sensational stuff, even without the authority of the episcopate. The language matched the occasion, as when the Bishop, doffing his mitre to the boys of "Beyond the Fringe," observed, "Only in the private world of the individual's psychological need and insecurity—in that last corner of 'the sardine-tin of life'—is room apparently left for God." It was the episcopal word with the common touch.

"Our Image of God Must Go" was some of the lava of the book, I discovered upon getting it on the appointed Tuesday and reading it; "Honest to God" was intended to be nothing less than a volcano. To me, just as to many others at the time, the story of Bonhoeffer—or, rather, what there was of it—was not unfamiliar. A theologian of great promise, he had been robbed of life at the age of thirty-nine, before he had been able to achieve his full powers, remaining, therefore, a shadowy figure who could just be glimpsed in his many books, which, considered together, presented a man grappling with ideas, profound but disturbing and only half-born, and showed a person hedged about with contradictions, such as those to be found in "Letters and Papers from Prison." In any case, that book, as the Bishop said, might be one of those trickles that split rocks a hundred years hence; "Honest to God" was an attempt to shatter them now. Though it was a five-shilling paperback, only a hundred and forty pages long, it immediately established itself as a popular classic. (Within a few weeks of its publication, a number of translators were at work on editions for Germany, Sweden, Denmark, and the Netherlands, and soon the Bishop and his publishers, the Student Christian Movement Press, of London, were collecting reviews and readers' letters, to be included, along with the Bishop's second thoughts, in another book, called "The Honest to God Debate," for by this time "Honest to God" had sold three hundred and fifty thousand copies, which were proclaimed a record for any "book of serious theology in the history of the world." Now the combined world sales have almost touched a million, which will probably stand as a record in the history of the world for some time to come.)

The argument of "Honest to God" went something like this: Once upon a time, men, including the writers of the New Testament, believed in a three-decker universe of Heaven, earth, and Hell—a belief that enabled them to speak and write about God as "up there." When, under the first onslaught of science, this universe collapsed, the loss was easily borne by a mere shift in verbal notation. God "up there" was amended to God "out there." This little tinkering with the spatial metaphor left the New Testament story intact and at the same time extricated Christianity from the flat-earth cosmology. Then came the Copernican onslaught—the dislodgment of the geocentric universe in favor of the heliocentric—which tended to make nonsense of God "out there." But some men, quickly coming to terms with this revolution in science, were able to go on thinking about God as in some way "beyond" outer space, perhaps because any further tinkering with the spatial metaphor might bring about an outright denial of the existence of God. The recent spying into space with radio telescopes and rockets, however, had dealt the coup de grâce to God "out there" and eliminated any other site where He might be supposed to have erected His house of many mansions. Along with Bonhoeffer, Rudolf Bultmann, an emeritus professor of theology at the University of Marburg, and the late Paul Tillich, who taught theology at (among other places) Union Theological Seminary and the Divinity Schools of Harvard and the University of Chicago, were among a number of modern Protestant theologians who had long since accepted the death of this God, who had accordingly set about modernizing Christianity, and who had commended themselves to the Bishop on these counts as soon as he happened to read them.

Bultmann, for his part, acknowledged that the New Testament writers presented Christ as a divine being—for example, as incarnated through a miraculous birth, as performing signs and wonders in testimony to his celestial origins, and as supranaturally redeemed and resurrected—but he asserted that these categories of preëxistence and incarnation, descent and ascent, miraculous intervention and cosmic catastrophe were mythological, and, for us today, were as primitive in their philosophy as the Book of Genesis was in its science. They belonged to a completely antiquated world view, he maintained, and, even when it was current, were used not to describe a supranatural event of any kind but to give expression to the real depth and significance—the "trans-historical" character—of the historical Jesus of Nazareth. Bultmann asserted, moreover, that Christianity was not committed to any mythological or supranaturalist picture of the world. Instead, according to him, it was today in need of a thoroughgoing "program of demythologization," not because all myths and symbols ought to be spurned but because Christianity had to sever its dependence on one particular mythology of supranaturalism. The difficulties and the consequences of the program were nowhere more evident than in its application to the doctrine of the Incarnation—the subject of many heresies and debates—which, at least in popular Christianity, had always stated that two distinct natures, that of God and that of man, were united in the person of Christ, or, in the words of Charles Wesley's hymn, "Veiled in flesh the Godhead see." But here, as elsewhere, Bultmann's answer was to read the Nativity story without supposing that its validity depended on a literal interruption of the natural order by a supranatural occurrence. Indeed, in his view, naturalism—the attempt to explain Christ's doings, like everything else, by humanistic and rational presuppositions—could alone claim the allegiance of intelligent men today.

Tillich's approach to the post-Copernican problem was somewhat different, the Bishop explained. For him, God was not a projection "out there," an Other, of whose reality we had to convince ourselves, but was within us, the very "ground of our being," "the deepest springs of our social and historical existence." As Tillich also put it, and the italics are his, "The name of this infinite and inexhaustible ground of history is *God*. That is what the word means, and it is that to which the words *Kingdom of God* and *Divine Providence* point. And if these words do not have much meaning for you, translate them, and speak of the depth of history, of the ground and aim of our social life, and of what you take seriously without reservation in your moral and political activities. Perhaps you should call this depth *hope,* simply hope. For if you find hope in the ground of history, you are united with the great prophets who were able to look into the depth of their times, who tried to escape it, because they could not stand the horror of their visions, and who yet had the strength to look to an even deeper level and there to discover hope." By reading "depth" for "height" in the Biblical imagery, and thus, in a sense, reversing the terms of the spatial metaphor, Tillich tried to give the Christian symbols relevance and meaning. God, instead of being conceived of as "the highest Being," was now defined as the depth of personal relationships—indeed, the depth of *all* experience "interpreted by love"—and, accordingly, theological statements were to be used to analyze this experience rather than to describe a supreme person. Similarly, Bonhoeffer spoke of God as "the 'beyond' in our midst." He began his reinterpretation of the Christian message where Bultmann had left off, and maintained that the traditional conception of God as a *deus ex machina* was as obsolete as the rest of Bultmann's myths. Man-come-of-age had no need to resort to the God hypothesis; in fact, it was a hindrance rather than a help to anyone trying to understand the workings of nature. Bonhoeffer would have agreed with Julian Huxley's remark "Operationally, God is beginning to resemble not a ruler but the last fading smile of a cosmic Cheshire Cat," but, unlike Huxley, Bonhoeffer chose to keep the Gospel and jettison only "Christianity" as "a pattern of religion." He died, however, before he could develop further this idea of "religionless Christianity."

To the Bishop, the ideas of Bultmann, Tillich, and Bonhoeffer, taken together, amounted to nothing less than a new Christianity; they suggested a radical reinterpretation of every Christian doctrine. Heaven was now conceived of as "the union-in-love with the ground of our being," this union being exemplified in Jesus Christ. Hell was "union-in-estrangement with the ground of our being"—a form of union exemplified by a sense of failure in coming to terms with oneself and others. Sin was "the abyss of separation" from that "ground of our being," as when one despaired. Grace was an offer of "life, in all its divine depth, to overcome the estrangement and alienation" from, again, that "ground of our being." The last thing the Church was intended to be was an organization for religious men. The motto for believers, in the new Christianity, was, more or less, "Hold to Christ, and for the rest be totally uncommitted," or, in the words of St. Augustine, "Love God, and do what you like." Indeed, the function of worship was to "sharpen and deepen our response to the world and to other people beyond the point of proximate concern (of liking, self-interest, limited commitment, etc.)," and the function of Holy Communion was to proclaim symbolically that Christ and "the beyond" were at the center of life. In the realm of ethics, similarly, the moral precepts of Christ were under no circumstances to be regarded as legislative, setting down courses of action universally right or wrong. On the contrary, they were to be taken as illustrations of what love might at any time require of anyone, the thing to remember in this case being that the Christian ethic was "a radical 'ethic of the situation,' with nothing prescribed—except love."

To look at only one instance of the application of the new morality, the sacrament of marriage was not to be taken as a union made in Heaven, and thus as possessing any metaphysical quality, but as something relative to the particular relationship, the particular situation. In this ethic of the situation, there was not even any hard and fast Christian rule about sexual experience before marriage, since there was nothing intrinsically evil except lack of love. But how was one to set about telling the believers from the non-believers? Here, as elsewhere—in fact, throughout the book—the Bishop left one in no doubt that he wanted to have things both ways. Though he had said that divorce and premarital sex experience were not in themselves wrong, he nevertheless insisted that they might be wrong "in 99 cases or even 100 cases out of 100." This was actually prejudging the situational ethic. The radical thinking, it turned out, was rooted, if not in the church of the Pharisees, in something pretty close to it. The Bishop even tried to narrow whatever gap might exist, on the chance that any Christian should take it into his head that his was the hundredth case. "To the young man asking in his relations with a girl, 'Why shouldn't I?'" the Bishop wrote, "it is relatively easy to say 'Because it's wrong' or 'Because it's a sin'—and then to condemn him when he, or his whole generation, takes no notice. It makes much greater demands to ask, and to answer, the question 'Do you love her?' or *'How much* do you love her?' and then to help him to accept *for himself* the decision that, if he doesn't, or doesn't very deeply, then his action is immoral, or, if he does, then he will respect her far too much to use her or take liberties with her." The Bishop's attempts to disarm any would-be critics of his Januslike views were little more rigorous than what might be called the "respect-for" logic. For instance, his answer to the question "If God had no existence separate from nature, then was the new Christianity pantheistic?" was that pantheism allowed for no personal moral freedom, whereas the new Christianity was rooted in the ideas of personal choice and love. These were but the most obvious cases of muddled thinking that struck me as I read.

I had thought that the newspaper statements, in themselves brief and tantalizing, would gain somehow in substance when they were elaborated in "Honest to God," but they did not. The style of the book, like that of a schoolboy's composition, was showy—bulging and straining at almost every point with far-fetched analogies constructed for purposes of polemics: "The traditional supranaturalistic way of describing the Incarnation almost inevitably suggests that Jesus was really God almighty walking about on earth, dressed up as a man. . . . He looked like a man, he talked like a man, he felt like a man, but underneath he was God dressed up—like Father Christmas. [The episcopal word à la sardines.] However guardedly it may be stated, the traditional view leaves the impression that God took a space-trip and arrived on this planet in the form of a man." Here, the Bishop felt the need of a qualification: "I am aware that this is a parody, and probably an offensive one, but I think it is perilously near the truth of what most people—and I would include myself—have been brought up to believe at Christmas-time." This, however, carried little conviction, especially since in the next breath he was off again: "It [Incarnation] conjures up the idea of a divine substance being plunged in flesh and coated with it like chocolate or silver plating." Nevertheless, the Bishop sometimes appeared defensive, and this not only furnished a relief from the ordinarily heavy-handed writing but helped to make him seem a more sympathetic speaker. "I never seriously thought of being anything but a parson," he said in a peroration to a chapter, "and, however much I find myself instinctively a radical in matters theological . . . I have never really doubted the fundamental truth of the Christian faith. . . . I am well aware that much of what I shall seek to say will be seriously misunderstood, and will doubtless deserve to be. Yet I feel impelled to the point where I can no other. . . . It is . . . a matter . . . of groping forward, almost of being pushed from behind. All I can do is to try to be honest—honest to God and about God—and to follow the argument wherever it leads." At other times, however, he gave the impression of someone still chafing under the conventional demands of his faith. Though he had served the Church since his days at theological college, he clearly had not always enjoyed it. "I believe the experts [clerical variety] have induced in us a deep inferiority complex," he confessed apropos of his difficulty in praying. "I can testify to this most strongly from the time I spent in a theological college, both as a student and as a teacher. . . . Here one ought to be able to pray, if ever one could. . . . I discovered there what I can only describe as a freemasonry of silent, profoundly discouraged, underground opposition, which felt that all that was said and written about prayer was doubtless unexceptionable but simply did not speak to 'our' condition. . . . But nothing else was offered in its place, and to this day we have an inferiority complex. We dare not admit to others or to ourselves what non-starters we are." The fact was that the Bishop had many voices, and he talked in all of them in discussing his own theory of prayer, and, by implication, the spirit of his book: "I am one of those who find that all my thinking and writing comes to me through immersion in what I have to *do*. Indeed, it is largely only literally by the activity of writing, with pen in hand, that I can think at all. . . . Isolate myself from the world [as in a period of withdrawal for prayer], and there is no grist to the mill. But it is equally clear that it is not only the mills of God that grind slowly. Time, space, withdrawal, if only from the telephone, is necessary if any fruit is to be brought to perfection. . . . It is then [in immersion in action] if ever, in this incarnational relationship, that deep speaks to deep and the Spirit of God is able to take up our inarticulate groans and turn them into prayer." Above all, then, "Honest to God" and its newspaper harbinger were prayers—*cris de cœur*.

Perhaps initially because of the sensational headline "OUR IMAGE OF GOD MUST GO," or because the writer of the article printed below it happened to be a bishop, and one who was familiar to the British public (he had been in the news before), or because his subject was religion and there was a smell of *succès de scandale* about the forthcoming "Honest to God," or because its bald conclusions were published in a newspaper, or because there were people in the offices of that paper and others who thought the Bishop and his controversial God would make good copy for weeks to come, the reaction to the Bishop of Woolwich's article in the *Observer* was immediate and violent. It was an intellectual spectacle—a sort of entertainment, I have learned through the years, that the British delight in. The Bishop was arraigned for heresy in the columns of several national papers and in some of the provincial press as well. The tone of the proceedings was either laborious or light, yet the judges succeeded in raising some serious questions and in demonstrating beyond any doubt that the Bishop's ideas, in spite of the questionable literary quality of their presentation, were as revolutionary as he had all along said they were, and that his personal dilemma was analogous to that of Christianity in the twentieth century. One newspaper reported that his fellow-bishops, the lower clergy, and the laity were calling his ideas "dangerous," "wrongheaded," and "incoherent," and another bitterly remarked of "Honest to God" that it "has been extravagantly praised by many who are not in the least interested in the better expression of theological truth but rather in seeing to it that there shall be no theological truths to express." Still another fusty magistrate was inspired to call for a full-scale heresy hunt among the clergy. "What should happen to an Anglican bishop who does not believe in God?" he wrote. "This, I hold, is the condition of the Bishop of Woolwich as revealed in his paperback 'Honest to God,' and it raises, I maintain, a question of Church discipline which cannot be shirked without the gravest repercussions on the whole Anglican Communion." The gentleman on the bench at the London *Times,* choosing a more contemporary approach, called in the aid of Oscar Wilde, who, in turn, conjured up the doubting Thomas: " 'In the English Church a man succeeds not through his capacity for belief but through his capacity for disbelief. Ours is the only Church where the sceptic stands at the altar, and where Saint Thomas is regarded as the ideal apostle.' If it seems a little unkind to quote Oscar Wilde against a bishop who is obviously well-meaning, the justification must be the disturbance he seeks to cause sophisticated as well as simple Christian minds. . . . The picture [of someone praying to the Bishop's nonexistent Heaven] is so bizarre that perhaps the comment may be made of Dr. Robinson that was made of Auguste Comte: *'Une religion sans Dieu! Mon Dieu, quelle religion!'* "

Naturally, the paper at the center of the *cause célèbre* was the *Observer*. The Sunday following the appearance of the article, one of the best of the young English humorists, Michael Frayn, reported in its columns on a fictitious mass rally of OIGMGO—the Our Image of God Must Go Movement—in Trafalgar Square. The rally, it seemed, had been called to update the image of God, and was presided over by a Bishop of Twicester. Thanks to his fantastic gyrations, it was said, this Bishop was a director of a business, Christianity, of which "Honest to God" was a study explaining that sales were falling off and recommending, instead of the liquidation of the business, a new advertising campaign. In the words of Frayn's dispatch, "The article in these pages last week by the Bishop of Woolwich . . . 'shall light such a neon sign by God's grace in England as I trust shall never be put out.' Or so the Bishop of Twicester, the well-known progressive divine, will say this afternoon. [The guarded prophetic tone, the cool simile, and the inversion of the quotation and its tag were a fairly accurate forgery of the Bishop of Woolwich's own hand.] This is a moving moment for me, witnessing at the birth of OIGMGO. As I'm sure some of you know, I have always been a strong supporter of Oecumenical, or broadening, trends in the Church, and opposed to Oiccumenical, or overdemanding ones, and I'm deeply convinced that Oigmgogicalism is the most Oecumenical and anti-Oiccumenical development yet. . . . The ordinary man in the street simply doesn't believe it [in God, that is]. The Bishop of Woolwich's great breakthrough has been to point out that the ordinary man in the bishopric doesn't believe it either."

Ordinary men in the street mounted the soapbox provided by the letters column of the *Observer* and commented like a Greek chorus on the *hubris* of that bishopric:

What we have left is not worth having.

The Bishop of Woolwich, who was studying theology at a time when I was a carefree atheist, seems to me to be suffering from postponed adolescence.

I am wondering if the Bishop would demonstrate the courage of his convictions by adopting the suggestion . . . that he cease to accept a secure living from the Church whose main traditional doctrines he now repudiates, and cast his bread upon the waters of this secular world, which, in his opinion, is so mature as to be able to dispense with a "Father-God," and to look after itself.

It is good to read the Bishop of Woolwich saying that the images of God that are meaningful and helpful in our age are not necessarily meaningful or helpful, or even true, for another age. This is precisely the Unitarian objection to making the acceptance of creeds and dogmas an essential condition of Church membership.

But what exactly—apart from mystical language—is left of the Christian religion when God drops out of it? Here the Bishop's courage seems to fail him, for there is only one answer: humanism. Some may consider Dr. Robinson's suggestion that humanists should then become Christians a somewhat impudent one. Has it ever occurred to him that Christians should become humanists? The humanists got there first, after all.

The thesis expounded by the Bishop of Woolwich was expressed rather more succinctly by Lenin when he said that the Communist revolution would never succeed until the myth of God had been wiped from the minds of men.

It was a festive occasion, too, for everyone whom the *Observer* specially invited to come and take stock of its prize.

The Most Reverend Dr. Edwin Morris, Archbishop of Wales, was just plain incredulous of what he saw: "The Bishop makes no mention of man's need of grace, redemption, salvation. Modern man, it seems, has become not only the measure of things but also the measure of God. I see no Gospel in this doctrine," and "I should like to know how the Bishop performs the verbal gymnastics needed, say, when celebrating the Holy Communion, to translate the Prayer Book into the language expressive of his present views. It must be very exhausting. Fortunately, he does not have to do it audibly." The Reverend Dr. E. L. Mascall, Professor of Historical Theology at London University, was quite insulted by, among other things, the way *he,* as one Christian, was regarded: " 'Our whole mental image of God must undergo a revolution.' But what is this image? As he [the Bishop] describes it, it is a mere caricature of anything that any intelligent Christian has ever taken literally. . . . Having rejected these two images [of 'up there' and 'out there'], Dr. Robinson shows a quite naïve predilection for the equally spatial image of 'depth,' which he thinks will appeal to modern man with his interest in depth psychology. . . . He really ought not to ascribe this shattering discovery to Dr. Tillich; he could have found it equally in St. Augustine. . . . Much of what he says a theologian will recognise as platitude in the form of paradox." Dr. C. S. Lewis, the late Professor of Medieval and Renaissance English at Cambridge, made the same point with all the authority of a great student of popular Christianity: "I have never met any adult who replaced 'God up there' by 'God out there' in the sense 'spatially external to the universe.' If I said God is 'outside' or 'beyond' space-time, I should mean 'as Shakespeare is outside "The Tempest," ' *i.e.,* its scenes and persons do not exhaust his being. . . . He [the Bishop] draws a sharp distinction between asking 'Does God exist as a person?' and asking whether ultimate reality is personal. But surely he who says yes to the second question has said yes to the first? Any entity describable without gross abuse of language as God must be ultimate reality, and if ultimate reality is personal, then God is personal." And Antony Flew, Professor of Philosophy at the University of Keele, in Staffordshire, and rebel against Christianity, brought along—as one might have expected—the philosopher's stone, and pressed home the point that Lewis had made about the personal God. He began with a puzzling affirmation by the Bishop in "Honest to God" that "reality at its very deepest level is personal" and the Bishop's philosophically contradictory assertion that "this has nothing necessarily to do with positing the existence of a Person." To shore up that contradictory statement, the Bishop had invoked Tillich and his view that what is most deeply true about us and for us—"depth," that is—is what the word "God" means. Flew drove home with "If that is how the word 'God' is now to be used, then it is indeed going to be hard to be an atheist: 'For,' as Tillich says, 'if you know that God means depth . . . you cannot then call yourself an atheist or unbeliever. For you cannot think or say: "Life has no depth!"' This is one short way with dissent." Flew then brilliantly stood the Bishop and his mentor on their heads: "But does Dr. Robinson appreciate that it must make Tillich's theology, in all but Tillich's own peculiar sense, atheist? For he—and no doubt Tillich, too—is also dedicated to the convictions: 'that . . . there is "nothing, in death or life . . . nothing in all creation that can separate us from the love of God in Christ Jesus our Lord"'; that under the regularities of nature 'and giving ultimate significance to them, is the yet deeper reliability of an utterly personal Love.' What can these claims mean, and how could they be true, if they are not to involve the sort of view earlier rejected so vigorously? Perhaps they could be 'reinterpreted' as simply a special sort of exhortation, or an affirmation of merely human possibilities. But Dr. Robinson rejects this option both in the article and, more clearly, in the book: 'The Christian affirmation is not simply that love *ought to be* the last word about life, but that, despite all appearances, it *is*.' Dr. Robinson seems to want both to refuse his cake and have it."

Probably the rebuke that stung the Bishop, as a clergyman, most painfully came on television from the Most Reverend and Right Honorable Arthur Michael Ramsey, Archbishop of Canterbury: ". . . When the Bishop goes on to say that God is 'deep down' and we must think of God in depth, I would say that I have always done that. I have always believed and have always taught all through my time that God is deep down as well as beyond. . . . When the ordinary Christian speaks of God as being 'up there' or of God 'being beyond,' he does not literally mean that God is in a place beyond the bright blue sky. He's putting in poetic language, which is the only service-able language we have, that God is supreme. . . . I think he is right when he is trying to find whether some new mode of the image of God may be going to help some of the people who are right outside Christianity and the Church, but it is utterly wrong and misleading to denounce the imagery of God held by Christian men, women, and children; imagery that they've got from Jesus himself, the image of God the Father in Heaven, and to say that we can't have any new thought until it is all swept away." But in a subsequent booklet he wrote on "Honest to God," entitled "Image Old and New," the Primate of All England seemed inclined to restore the fallen Bishop: "We state and commend the faith only in so far as we go out and put ourselves with loving sympathy inside the doubts of the doubting, the questions of the questioners, and the loneliness of those who have lost their way. . . . We need to see if there are some who are helped by thinking not about God above us in heaven, or even God around and near, but about the deep-down meaning of human life in terms of love. There may be those who find there the heart of the matter: and this *is* God, even though a man may not be able to cry with Thomas, 'My Lord

and my God.' " But as the dispute kept on gathering throughout England, like a tempest, the Primate seemed to be tossed
about by the contrary winds. His booklet had not been out for
much more than a week when, in a presidential address to the
Convocation of Canterbury, he stiffened again: "I was specially
grieved at the method chosen by the Bishop for presenting his
ideas to the public. We are asked to think that the enterprise
was a matter of being 'tentative,' 'thinking aloud,' 'raising questions,' and the like. But the initial method chosen was a newspaper article, crystal clear in its argument and provocative in its
shape and statement, to tell the public that the concept of a
personal God as held both in popular Christianity and in orthodox doctrine is outmoded and that atheists and agnostics are
right to reject it. Of course, the association of this thesis with a
Bishop of the Church caused public sensation and did
much damage."

The most cursory reading of theological and lay writings made
it clear that this thesis, to which, according to the Primate,
Bishop Robinson had so flagrantly lent his name, had its roots
among some of the leading Christian thinkers in Europe and
America. There was hardly a major center of Christian study
in any part of the world where the thought of Bultmann,
Tillich, and Bonhoeffer was not being daily expounded and
interpreted by these theologians' pupils and disciples, many of
whom, distinguished theologians in their own right, had also
been meeting regularly for some years to discuss the latest
developments in what was generally known as "the new theology." Nor was the ferment mainly German; the English, while
spurning Teutonic categories of thought as a matter of course,
were in the middle of a little revolution of their own, although,
naturally, there were many theologians who were going along
quite obliviously in their old ways. Their chief organ, the
Journal of Theological Studies, was filled with such articles as

"Scientific Hermeneutics According to St. Thomas Aquinas" and "An Eighth-Century Melkite Colophon from Edessa" and "A Lost Hebrew Word in Isaiah II: 6." A group of "iconoclastic" Anglican clergy had, within the space of a few months, convened twice at Keble College, Oxford, and the papers read at the first conference had been collected and published under the title "Layman's Church." Typical of the collection was the article by Canon Douglas Rhymes, of Southwark Cathedral, advocating "holy worldliness," with which clerics were somehow to take their faith outside the Church and put it to use in their secular environment. John Wren-Lewis, an Imperial Chemical Industries official and lay theologian, was writing elsewhere—in the Anglican monthly *Prism,* to be precise—on why it was sometimes better not to go to church, and also, in the *Guardian,* about modern Biblical scholarship, which had shown, for instance, that "the famous parable of the sheep and the goats . . . says nothing whatever about life after death, and the judgment it describes is not of individuals but of *nations,*" and that "it tells us the *nations* that have cared for the hungry and afflicted are blessed, while the nations that have neglected to do so are accursed: if we want to apply it in modern terms, it is a demand for Welfare States rather than for strained individual virtue." Around the same time, Werner Pelz, a European refugee who had become a vicar in Lancashire, surprised Britons with a book, which I found unreadable, called "God Is No More." Indeed, back in 1962, before "Honest to God" erupted on the island, about a dozen dons and professors, mostly from Cambridge, where the Bishop himself had once been a student and then a tutor, had published "Soundings: Essays Concerning Christian Understanding," a rather uneven work that, growing out of years of study and conversation among the contributors, tried to evaluate Christianity in the present day. In the disarming opening words of its editor, A. R. Vidler, Fellow and Dean of King's College, "The authors of this volume of essays cannot persuade themselves that the time is ripe for major works of theological construction or reconstruction. It is a time for ploughing, not reaping; or, to use the metaphor we have chosen for our title, it is a time for soundings, not charts or maps." But the body of the book almost belied its modest presentation, as when H. A. Williams, Fellow and Dean of Trinity College, after commenting at some length on how the prostitute in the Greek film "Never on Sunday" commits a Christian act of charity by taking to bed a sailor who lacks confidence in his "capacity for physical union" (that recalcitrant one case out of a hundred), went on to consider the theological implications of another film—an English one, this time—called "The Mark." He wrote, "It tells of the rehabilitation into normality of a man strongly attracted to small girls. His abnormality, which can do nothing but untold harm to everybody, is due to his fear of commitment to an adult woman. However, in time, a woman of his own age inspires him with enough confidence for them to go away for a weekend together. They have separate rooms at the hotel. But it is clear that until he sleeps with her he will not have established enough confidence in himself to deliver him from his utterly destructive abnormality, which tends to exploitation to the nth degree. Will he be able to summon up the necessary courage or not? When he does, and they sleep together, he has been made whole. And where there is healing, there is Christ, whatever the Church may say about fornication. And the appropriate response is—Glory to God in the Highest. Yet each of the men in these two films might have disguised his fear by the cloak of apparent morality. Like the Pharisees in the Gospels and many good churchmen today, they might have been the victims of unconscious hypocrisy, keeping the law as an insulation against the living God, the Creator." The book sometimes left an impression of intelligent Anglicans sunk so deep in the sea of Christian thought that one could only wonder if there was any bottom to it.

I naturally looked forward to further soundings. Within two weeks of the unveiling of "Honest to God," four members of the Cambridge Faculty of Divinity—Professor D. M. MacKinnon, of Corpus Christi, and J. S. Bezzant, Fellow and Dean of St. John's, and Vidler and Williams, three of them described as High Churchmen—were in print with "Objections to Christian Belief," on this occasion with the avowed claim that the case against Christianity could not be met by "the mere repetition of old arguments," since the primary need was to understand "as clearly and deeply as possible what the fundamental objections to Christian belief now are." The book, which had an essay from each of the four authors, dealing with moral, intellectual, psychological, or historical objections, was in fact a collection of lectures that had been delivered at the university and subsequently mulled over by student groups—circumstances that gave it such a prepublication impetus that it was easily able to ride indefinitely, piggyback fashion, on the sales of "Honest to God," and later itself provoked and helped to sell two companion volumes: "Objections to Roman Catholicism," a combined effort by several Catholic clergymen and laymen, and "Objections to Humanism," by a group of professed humanists. A *Guardian* editorial remarked that "anyone who still supposes that Dr. Robinson is out on a solitary limb would be well advised to read . . . 'Objections to Christian Belief,' " and how all these Christians managed to balance themselves on that crowded limb was made fairly clear in the essays by two earlier "Soundings" contributors. Vidler, pointing out that Christianity was a historical faith in the sense that it seemed to stand or fall, in Professor Mascall's words, "by certain events that were alleged to have taken place during a particular period of forty-eight hours in Palestine nearly two thousand years ago," and then raising formidable objections to Christianity as a faith, going as far as to question the existence of Jesus Himself, tried at the same time to maintain that one could be a Christian in spite of these obstacles. He wrote:

First, I would call your attention to a fundamental objection to any tie-up between Christian belief and alleged historical events or the existence of an historical person. . . . [This] objection was expressed by the Mahatma Gandhi in an address . . . "I may say that I have never been interested in an historical Jesus. I should not care if it was proved by some one that the man called Jesus never lived, and that what was narrated in the Gospels was a figment of the writer's imagination. For the Sermon on the Mount would still be true for me." . . . [People like Mahatma Gandhi] considered that Christian belief ought to be about the teaching, not the person, of Jesus. They considered that Jesus happened to enunciate certain spiritual and moral truths, ideals or principles the validity of which was independent of his own person or circumstances. . . . I fancy that there are a great many ordinary Christian believers who, if they were articulate, would confess that it is the *practical* implications of Christian belief which are of decisive importance for them, and not the historical origins or the *speculative* implications. . . . [Historical statements involved in Christian belief] are not matters of universal agreement: in fact, the early Christians were regarded as mad because they believed them, and it has often been so since. . . . It is well enough known that the experts—those who have made themselves competent to form an opinion of their own about Christian origins—differ very widely in their conclusions. There have even been learned and intelligent men who have denied that Jesus ever existed: the so-called "Christ-myth" theory.

But one soon sensed that Vidler, like the Bishop, wanted both to refuse his cake and to have it.

It seems reasonable, and indeed inevitable, that a man's judgment about the origins of Christianity—where the evidences in the narrower sense are manifestly susceptible of more than one interpretation—should be influenced by his assessment of the total Christian phenomenon in history. . . . So that, finally, I would say that the way in which a Christian believer responds, in the last resort, to the historical objections to Christian belief which we have been considering is likely to be settled by one or both of two things, which are not unrelated. On the one hand, by the enduring impression or impact that is made upon him by the person of Jesus as he is portrayed in the Gospels. . . . And, on the other hand, whether a man decides to become or to remain a Christian believer may also be settled by what I would call his participation in the Christian mystery as a present reality: by what he finds, or by what finds him, in the shared experience of the community of believers— it may be the eucharistic sacrament or in the Friends' meeting house: by whether or not he is convinced that there is something there which, despite all his puzzlements, holds him and speaks to the deepest levels of his being. This, I take it, is what Paul Tillich had in mind when he said: "The affirmation that Jesus is the Christ is an act of faith and consequently of daring courage. It is not an arbitrary leap into darkness but a decision in which elements of immediate participation and therefore certitude are mixed with elements of strangeness and therefore incertitude and doubt." . . . And here I might interject that I often find myself more in sympathy or en rapport with non-Christians who have a sense of the strangeness and incertitude of our world and of the duty of a large measure of agnosticism than I do with Christians who are cocksure about their belief.

Williams went further, if anything. Writing on the theme of psychological objections, he developed his concept of the conflict between (in his words) "what I once believed to be the essentials of Christianity" and "what I have discovered about the way I work as a human person, the subterranean forces and strategies of which I have become aware within"—a reference to Freud's discoveries and to some years Williams himself spent undergoing psychoanalysis. With the instrument of psychoanalysis, he went after the Church and what in his view was its cardinal error: "Let a person feel guilty enough, and he will do what he is told"—as in matters of sex and marriage. Williams went on to illustrate the inconsistency of the Church's dicta, asserting that many Christians living today believed that

Christ was present in a second marriage following divorce, yet at the turn of the century most Christians would have considered this belief anathema. In the interim, of course, the climate of opinion throughout our society had changed drastically. And yet Christ must have been equally present in a second marriage then, even if the Victorians were blind to His presence and blessing. In fact, Christians had an enormous stake—and Williams did not exclude himself from this—in rejecting Christ whenever He appeared in guises offensive to the prevailing social and moral attitudes, since they used God as (in Williams' characteristic figure) "the whitewash with which to paint the sepulchre where their own corruption lies concealed." At one point, he argued that if a Christian were possessed by guilt feelings he could even persuade himself that he was responding freely to God's love, with the result that the "good" people of a congregation stood in far greater danger of alienation from God's love than their seemingly degenerate brethren. In so turning the tables, Williams was led to contend that behind the façade of "much worship and good words" Christians unconsciously harbored "the demon of guilt feelings," and, whatever their intellectual or theological sophistication, they were caught in the demon's claws.

And Williams' analysis of the demon of guilt feelings made him embrace a Christianity more eccentric in some ways than that of the Bishop. He said that he had known an intelligent Anglican who had piously gone through the motions of conventional Christian devotion until a nightmare shook the foundations of his faith. In the nightmare, this man was watching a play when he happened to look around and see a grotesque puppeteer manipulating all the players on the stage through hypnosis. The man awoke from the dream in terror, and it took him some months to interpret the vision. In Williams' words:

The monster of the nightmare was the god he was really worshipping in spite of his having got a First in the Theological Tripos....

His dream showed him that he was a devil's slave—his devotion and his goodness being a compulsive response to a deeply embedded feeling of guilt, and this, in spite of his regular use of sacramental confession. It broke him up temporarily. But later he was certain that, although he was much less religious in the usual sense, he had been brought to the strait gate and the narrow way. For life and behavior based on feelings of guilt excludes charity. To be bullied, compelled, by subtle inner unidentifiable fear to apparent worship and goodness is to destroy the self. And without a self one cannot give. There can be no charity, no love for God or man. The dreamer whose history (with his permission) I have recounted was seen, about two years after his nightmare, drunk among the bars and brothels of Tangier. He was learning that for him evil was not what the priests had told him it was, but rather that evil was the disguised slavery to his own hidden corruption which had led him to go to Mass every day and to confession every month. And he told me that words of Jesus rang in his ears like bells of victory—the words which Jesus addressed to the churchmen of His day—"Verily I say unto you, that the publicans and the harlots go into the Kingdom of God before you."

This type of thinking made the writer Wayland Young quip, "Surely the only function of the new theology is to make premarital and extra-marital sex respectable." Most commentators, however, took the view that, as one of them put it, "we are today at the beginning of a considerable theological revolution which may well assume for this century the importance the Reformation had for Western Europe four hundred years ago." Some went as far as to contend that the revolution, this time, would not be limited to Western Europe, or to Protestantism, as it would even take in tow the Vatican, and, indeed, there were radical voices hailing from all corners of Christendom. There was, for instance, a fiery tongue over the head of the Episcopal Bishop of California, the Right Reverend James A. Pike, whose name was often linked with Robinson's, though

Pike sounded like an instructor in a department of which Robinson was the head. On the Roman Catholic front, Thomism and Neo-Thomism, the representatives of scholasticism and the predominant schools of thought in this century, were being edged aside as Catholic theologians tried to rethink, and find new language and concepts for, traditional problems. The messengers of this change included, among others, disciples of ecumenicity (which inevitably would involve a certain amount of doctrinal modernizing and horse-trading with the Protestants), and those, on the one hand, who would come to grips with the problem of secularization by developing the theological implications of Teilhard de Chardin's ideas (not, however, by recourse to Bonhoeffer and his notion about "religionless Christianity," since his influence was confined, as yet, only to the students at Catholic seminaries), and those, on the other, who would "desecularize" our world in order to rediscover the Christian meaning in it (the names that come first to mind in this connection are those of Father Hans Küng, in Tübingen, and Karl Rahner, S. J., who is a professor of dogmatic theology in Innsbruck and was an official theologian to the Second Vatican Council, which in time, it was hoped, would give rise to the "new" Church). The sixteenth- and seventeenth-century battles of the Reformation and the Counter Reformation might, in fact, it was thought, one day be forgotten in what Pope John XXIII called and proclaimed the era of a "new Pentecost."

As controversy still whirled about the Bishop, I turned eagerly to "The Honest to God Debate," which was in and out of the bookstalls with almost the speed of "Honest to God," in the hope of finding some sort of resolution. Because the Bishop was such an easy mark for criticism, and the comments of his detractors had been so abundant, making so many points (some of them off the top of the head), and yet the congregation at large had been so nearly silent, one felt in need of a leisurely retrospective view, together with additional lay comment—particularly as it became clear that the Bishop was not just crying in an intellectual wilderness. "The Honest to God Debate," a selective compilation of articles on "Honest to God," letters to the Bishop, and essays written for the book by various clerics and laymen, was intended to satisfy this need, but it succeeded only in exacerbating it. It appeared too soon after "Honest to God," it suffered from being edited indulgently and ponderously by the Reverend David L. Edwards, managing director and chief editor of the Bishop's publishers, and, as a book, it seemed to lack direction and clarity, even allowing for the divergence of style and content to be expected in such a collection. Still, the book *was* about "Honest to God."

A chapter, written by the Bishop, that dealt largely with his critics appeared calculated to appease the howling winds. He wrote, temporizing, "The issues raised by the debate, theoretical and practical, are too big to be taken up so soon or within the scope of an essay, and the atmosphere at some points is still too emotionally charged." He took shelter behind rigmarole: "My original title [for the *Observer* article] 'A New Mutation in Christianity?' was designed to be positive and to draw attention to the contribution of Dietrich Bonhoeffer. . . . The one suggested to me [by the *Observer*]—'Our Image of God Must Go'—struck me as negative and arrogant. I resisted it, but under pressure of time and with nothing convincing to propose in its place, I eventually concurred. Journalistically it was a good title, as events were to show. But as well as leaving a destructive impression, it also had the effect of shifting the centre of gravity of the subsequent debate." He covered his tracks with begged questions: "The initiative for . . . [the article] came entirely from the staff of the *Observer* and presented (at short notice) what I still believe was a real opportunity outside the normal channels of the Church to engage at a serious level as a Christian in the intellectual debate of our day. Whether I used the opportunity aright must be left to others to judge." In fact, he proved himself in the "Debate" to be fluent in diversionary talk from both sides of his mouth: "The important thing is that what is history is not more true because it is history nor what is myth less true because it is myth. . . . But it is essential to see the myth for what it is, and not simply to say that the Christian myths are true because 'they happened.' "

The other contributors to the "Debate" were more straightforward, as when the Right Reverend Arthur Mervyn Stockwood, the Diocesan Bishop of Southwark—to whom Robinson is a suffragan—tried to polish up the somewhat battered name of his assistant: "I have known John Robinson for twenty years. He has proved himself a faithful pastor, a fearless thinker, and a dynamic Christian. Although I cannot pretend to keep abreast of his thinking, there is no man in the Church for whose mind I have a greater admiration or for whose integrity and single-minded devotion I have more respect. I have read 'Honest to God' three times, and it has taught me much." The Bishop of Southwark was grandly assisted by Rudolf Bultmann, one of the masters on whose work Robinson had drawn so heavily. In a review from *Die Zeit,* reprinted in the "Debate," Bultmann professorially advised all those who would shrug the Bishop aside as old hat to exercise forbearance: "One may say that for many people, especially for German theologians, the author's intention, and often its achievement in detail, are not new. . . . Yet it seems to me very unjust when German voices, as far as they have come to my knowledge, say rather lightly, 'Nothing new for us!' For the book deserves all respect as evidence of an attempt to wrestle with the problems involved in the situation, and the author is entitled to ask us to consider his ideas conscientiously. And is our situation really so enlightened, and have the relevant problems been so finally solved, that there is no need for them to be constantly thought out afresh?"

For an ordinary reader, the most novel part of the "Debate"

was the section containing letters—mainly from laymen. Most hostile letters had been excluded, so the published correspondence gave a somewhat one-sided impression. The letters came from writers described anonymously as "a colonel," "a civil engineer," "a schoolteacher," "an English doctor," "a professor of medicine," "a professor of mathematics," "a businessman," "a well-known politician," "a man in the street," "a woman of twenty," "an undergraduate at Oxford," "a woman of 83," "an old lady," "a woman from Devon," "a woman from Canterbury," "a vicar's wife," "a woman's voice from the vicarage," "a voice from the pews," "a less faithful churchgoer," "an archdeacon," "a priest," "a doctor who might have been a priest," and so on, and despite their variety, almost every one of them saw in the mirror of "Honest to God" the reflection of his own emotions, most of the confessions reading along the lines of the following:

May I quote to you from one of Dannie Abse's poems which seems so well to express this need and inability to accept the popular image?

> "Dear God in the end You had to go.
> Dismissing You, Your absence made us sane.
> We keep the bread and wine for show . . .
>
> "And still our dark declensions sorrow
> That grape is but grape and grain is grain.
> We keep the bread and wine for show."

So many of our poets and writers are writing this way—but they cannot leave the source of their creative power; however they stretch and pull at the umbilical cord it draws them back again, until like T. S. Eliot and Thomas Blackburn they "break through" the veil of reasoned disillusion and the outworn creeds of man's convenience.

And:

I have a deep inner desire to return to church, which I find I can satisfy by attending church services abroad where I can understand nothing of the message, yet can be reminded by the environment and by the deeply reverent attitudes of the worshippers, as well as by the magnificent music and the religious pictures, of the intention behind the ritual, and of the deep religious experiences I used to feel as a boy. So often I find myself wishing I had never grown up.

The most interesting essays came from the hand of David Jenkins, Fellow and Chaplain of Queen's College, Oxford, and Alasdair MacIntyre, Fellow of University College, Oxford. Though MacIntyre was the more single-minded and relentless in argument, both scholars were bent on pinning a charge of intellectual atheism on the Bishop, and—sometimes implicitly but most of the time explicitly—on Bultmann, Tillich, and Bonhoeffer as well. Indeed, the spectre of intellectual atheism—raised earlier by Flew, among other critics—had been stalking these theologians all along. According to Jenkins, Robinson's attempt "to be honest to God is so dishonest to the God of, for example, Athanasius or the fourth century Cappadocian writers or of Thomas Aquinas, let alone Augustine or, again, to the God of the author of the 'Cloud of Unknowing' or, say, to the God who is worshipped in and through the shape of the Orthodox Liturgy, that it is clearly high time that we were confronted by an explosive reminder of the need to 'get our theism right.'" Jenkins' examination was built around such questions as: Is the "ultimate reality" of Tillich and Robinson any more objective than the traditional God they reject? Or, alternatively, is the experience of "ultimate reality" more self-evident and objective than the awareness of the traditional God? And aren't Tillich and Robinson guilty of some legerdemain when, in their eagerness to prevent "ultimate reality" from becoming simply a subjective experience, they claim for it a sort of objective status and then surreptitiously endow it with personal attributes? When Robinson asserted that often in debates between Christians and humanists his sympathies were on the humanists' side, he saw fit to explain: "This is not in the least because my faith or commitment is in doubt." The difficulty that Jenkins found with this was "For me, 'faith' implies 'faith in' and 'commitment' implies 'commitment to.' I do not think this is just a question of language—or, alternatively, if it is, it is a point to be followed up because, in one sense, the whole discussion is about language—about how we should talk and have grounds for talking about 'ultimate realities.'" Jenkins next turned to Tillich, who had said, "The first step to atheism is always a theology which drags God down to the level of doubtful things." While admitting that this might be so, Jenkins went on to develop the main line of his argument:

I very much fear that there is a real sense in which the existence of God is doubtful (i.e., capable of being doubted), that atheism will always seem a real existential possibility, and that this remains so even if you attempt to restate the doctrine of God in terms of "ultimate concern" and the like. In this connection a remark of the Bishop's is very instructive: "God is, by definition, ultimate reality. And one cannot argue whether ultimate reality exists." We have, I think, detected some very determinedly anti-traditional-metaphysic thinkers trying to get away with a concealed and possibly inverted version of the traditional ontological argument. (This is the argument that the *idea* of God includes the idea of existing and so God *must* exist. The mistake in this has usually been supposed to be that while the *idea* of God may include the *idea* of existing the fact that people have *ideas* of a certain sort is, of itself, no evidence at all that anything corresponding to the ideas *really* exists.) Of course you cannot argue whether ultimate reality exists. You can only ask whether pretentious phrases like "ultimate reality" are wanted at all and, *a fortiori*, whether there is any case for bringing the word "God" within smelling distance of the argument. Moreover the "ultimate reality" or "ultimate concern" of Robinson and of Tillich (in the quotations Robinson uses) is no more an obvious, self-evident or demonstrably necessary feature of the world or of our experiences in the world than God is. Thus Robinson continues the passage I have just referred to: ". . . one cannot argue whether ultimate reality exists. One can only ask what ultimate reality is like. . . ." It is quite clear that the answer he wishes to maintain as the true answer to *that* question is by no means self-evident, and if it is not self-evident it is, of course, doubtful and deniable (like the God of the theism he is wondering whether to repudiate). For example, on p. 49 he writes: "To believe in God as love means to believe that in pure personal relationship we encounter, not merely what ought to be, but what is, the deepest, veriest truth about the structure of reality. This, in face of all the evidence, is a tremendous act of faith. But it is not the feat of persuading oneself of the existence of a super-Being beyond this world endowed with personal qualities. Belief in God is the trust, the well-nigh incredible trust, that to give ourselves to the uttermost in love is not to be confounded but to be 'accepted,' that Love is the ground of our being, to which ultimately we 'come home.' " "In face of all the evidence," "the well-nigh incredible trust" and so on make it quite clear that talk about the existence of ultimate reality not being arguable is irrelevant bluff. "Ultimate reality" is a trivial and meaningless phrase until you begin to characterize "it," and the character the Bishop (and Tillich) want to give "it" is something over and above "it" where "it" is just plain matter of fact reality (the "stuff" that is "all the evidence"). . . . But the logical difficulties of theism are not even clarified, let alone removed by their procedure. Indeed a good deal of the language seems in danger of being less clear and, thereby, possibly more dishonest than some more traditional statements. Take, for example, the extended quote from Tillich on p. 81, where the talk is of grace. Grace is carefully referred to as "it," but "it" behaves in a very personal way (and, indeed, since the "happenings" involved are said not to be at our command it looks very much as if grace "comes in from outside"—at any rate from outside us). The situation referred to is "as though a voice were saying 'You are accepted.' " Now "seeming to be addressed" and still more "accepting the fact that we are accepted" sound like descriptions of a personal relationship with a being who is at least personal and we may perhaps believe that that *is* what is being pointed to, as later on the term "Ground" gets a capital "G," which suggests that perhaps it is being treated as very like a proper name. . . . I should maintain, therefore, that the traditional theistic talk about a personal God is no more (although admittedly no less) *logically* difficult than is the talk about "ultimate reality" and "ultimate concern" which is urged upon us. For *as used* the term "ultimate reality" no more refers to some self-evident existence than does the name "God."

MacIntyre went further. Not only Tillich and Robinson were atheist in substance but also Bultmann and Bonhoeffer, even though all of them continued to use a theistic vocabulary. In fact, his article, entitled "God and the Theologians," which, because of some publishing vagary, was reproduced in truncated form in the "Debate," was so sweeping that I found myself compelled to look up the fuller version, originally printed in *Encounter*. His bombardment was directed at the sources of the Bishop's wide appeal. As one source he distinguished two varieties of atheism. The first variety he described as "speculative atheism, which is concerned to deny that over and above the universe there is something else . . . and in general to expose religion as a series of intellectual mistakes." The second, he said, involved the assumption that "religion needs to be translated into non-religious terms and not simply rejected." MacIntyre insisted that the Bishop was atheist on both counts, then wrote:

Yet I think that we might well be puzzled by this strong desire for a theological vocabulary; for the only reason given for preserving the name "God" is that "our being has depths which naturalism, whether evolutionary, mechanistic, dialectical, or humanistic, cannot or will not recognize." . . . And that our accounts of human nature are all inadequate, most atheists would concede. But what, according to the Bishop, is at issue *is* how to describe *our* nature and not anything else. . . . The response to his book might suggest that the combination of a religious vocabulary with substantial atheism has a wide appeal. And this is a second reason why "Honest to God" may be important. . . . The liberal idealism, which easily confused a secular faith in uninterrupted progress with belief in the actions of a divine providence could not survive the trenches of World War I. Tillich was an army chaplain, as Bultmann was to be later on. [Actually, Bultmann was never an army chaplain.] Bonhoeffer was to be executed by the Nazis. The problem of evil had to be more than an academic exercise. Moreover, the matter of traditional Protestant preaching, with its moralizing and its promise of pietistic consolations, could scarcely survive. Two questions pressed in: How can we think of God after the Somme, after Auschwitz? And how can we preach to contemporary man?

But this response to the evils of the Somme and Auschwitz was by no means the only one, and MacIntyre, by turning to an alternative that had been monumentally argued by Karl Barth, opened up a second front in his attack on the atheistic theologians:

The first answer to these questions was Barth's commentary on *Romans* ["The Epistle to the Romans"], where St. Paul's Greek is conjured into a blend of Luther, Calvin, Dostoevski, and Kierkegaard. (Not so misleading either, for each of them had digested large quantities of St. Paul.) Barth's message is that any attempt to justify belief in God or any attempt to comprehend God's ways by translating revelation into terms other than its own is bound to fail. God is infinitely distant from man and totally other. In revelation he condescends to us; we can only accept or reject, we cannot argue. Evil cannot be explained; but we can be redeemed and saved from its power. . . . And certainly as Barthian theology has developed systematically, it has remained a keystone of orthodoxy. . . . But Barthian theology nonetheless contains the materials for its own self-transformation. For if the Word of God cannot be identified with *any* frail human attempt to comprehend it, the way is open for sympathy with those who reject human theologies which have attempted to substitute for the Divine Word. . . . If it is *any* human work or word which we have to carefully avoid identifying or confusing with the divine, then we are in a very different position from that of traditional Protestant pietistic orthodoxy. For none but God can be infallible; and hence no church authority, and not even the scriptures, can be treated as infallible without impiety. This was the basis upon which Barth welcomed radical, scholarly criticism of the New Testament while fundamentalist orthodoxy always rejected it. . . . At this point, therefore, Protestant theology has had to face up to its own inadequacies.

MacIntyre now addressed himself to Bultmann, Tillich, and Bonhoeffer individually:

Bultmann's theology has three quite separate elements to it. There is first of all his historical scepticism about the New Testament events. Closely connected with this is his belief that the New Testament message is presented in terms of a pre-scientific cosmology and that consequently the gospel must be "de-mythologized" before it can be preached to scientific man. And there is, thirdly, his view of what the de-mythologized message in fact is. . . . This mythology conceals rather than conveys the message that man is a prey to an inauthentic existence, that Jesus summons him to a decision, by which he can face up to his being as that of one who is going to die and so begin to live authentically. . . . When the gospel is de-mythologized, a theistic existentialism is what remains. But is this existentialism more than nominally theistic? Bultmann's pupil [Wilhelm] Kamlah took the final step of pointing out that what Bultmann takes the life of faith to be makes its possibility logically independent of the occurrence of any event in Palestine in the first century and, indeed, of the existence of a supernatural being. . . . Tillich's contrast with Bultmann is at first sight sharp. ". . . if you know that God means depth, you know much about him. You cannot then call yourself an atheist or unbeliever. For you cannot think or say: Life has no depth! Life is shallow!"

MacIntyre now blasted these much quoted lines from Tillich:

Clearly, however, the conversion of the unbeliever is only so easy for Tillich because belief in God has been evacuated of all its traditional content. . . . Even if we were to concede Tillich a verbal triumph over the atheist, the substance of atheism has been conceded.

Just as Bultmann's view of the New Testament points towards scepticism, so does Tillich's analysis of the doctrine of God.

Explaining that Bonhoeffer's Christianity was intelligible in only one context, that of the thirties in Europe and of Nazi Germany, where God and man were in a sense powerless, where the Christian role was reduced merely to one of suffering witness, and where, therefore, Bonhoeffer's God came to have special relevance, MacIntyre added:

Outside that context it lacks precisely any specific differentia from the way of life of sensitive, generous liberals. It does not issue in atheism as the conclusion of an argument (as Bultmann's theology does), and it does not present atheism in theological language (as Tillich's theology does), but it fails in the task for which it was designed and in our sort of society it becomes a form of practical atheism, for it clothes the ordinary liberal forms of life with the romantic unreality of a catacombic vocabulary.

The specific rebuttal that the Bishop made in the "Debate" to the charge of atheism levelled at him and his masters showed, at best, that even though MacIntyre had succeeded in cornering them intellectually, he had violated their spirit. Yet MacIntyre, who was perhaps a victim of that fashion among certain English intellectuals—particularly the breed of "don-journalists"—of going in for elementary socio-psychology, also failed in his task, since his explanation of why these learned men retained a theistic vocabulary while acquiring an atheistic substance amounted only to the contention that their ambivalence was due to the uneasy peace between theism and atheism existing today, as when people continue to be baptized, married, and buried in the church, even if they are actually non-believers.

In recent years in Britain, as the walls between classes have begun to collapse, and the élite and the populace have been more and more closely meshed into one attenuated and ever-expanding middle-class literate public, the press of both the masses and the classes, seeing a vast market to be exploited, has given intellectuals their head in prominent columns, with the result that the distinction between the two types of newspaper, once so marked, has itself tended to disappear. Apart from the sellers, the main beneficiaries of this trade have been the big cultural names—especially those with a polemical bent, a fast and easy pen, and an eye for the hemline in ideas on war and politics, sex and religion, or any other subject of general interest. The phenomenon is now so widespread that a casual visitor to Fleet Street, listening to the discussion of reputations, watching them be pumped up and punctured, might come away with the impression that the district was a financial exchange on which the stock of each intellectual was liable to sudden fluctuations in value. If one asks an editor, as I did on a visit to Fleet Street not long ago, about the pros and cons of the new system, the question is hardly taken seriously, so rapidly has the system become a part of the scene. However, one newspaperman, who, after some badgering, stopped to reflect, replied by dwelling almost entirely on the positive aspects of the new era. "We are living in the sixties and we might as well face it," he said. "The system is the child of democracy. People want to be up on intellectual things. It's a legitimate aspiration, which we have a duty to satisfy. We have a duty to air ideas with any public interest at all; that's just good journalism. And the more controversial the better; controversy keeps people interested, and another function of good journalism is to entertain. Besides, all these debates in the newspapers help to bring those rarefied dons and professors and bishops nearer to the public, just as they help to keep intellectuals in touch with the world by constantly subjecting their ideas to the test of common sense. British thinking has always had deep roots in common sense and empiricism, and if this has led to a certain amount of cheerful vulgarity—well, that, too, has been a part of British life. Also, sending off polemics, rebuttals, and criticisms is as healthy as cricket—it's a safety valve. It's been said that polemics, by definition, slant and exaggerate, but, in a sense, that can be said of any sort of writing."

That the system nevertheless has some unhealthy offshoots is undeniable. The controversies are often started up capriciously and then capriciously set aside. They are argued from so many different directions and at such heat that, most of the time, they tend to blur all lines of argument, with few points of view ever coinciding. After all, the forum *is* newspapers, not books; the aim is quixotic journalism, not intensive exploration; the game is more important than the outcome; and the disputes, of necessity, have to be spread thin, over many weeks and many disparate papers. No wonder any glimmerings of truth that emerge from the clash of ideas, any demonstrated rights and wrongs of the issue, are lost—simply swept under the editorial carpet with yesterday's news.

Whatever the merits of the system, no one can be entirely pleased with the way each debate is finally enshrined in memory. After the hurly-burly, its main participants and its victims become "controversial"—a designation that in its way is as tenacious as the title of duke or corporal, and much more meaningless. For his effort, the Bishop received that accolade (or raspberry, depending on how one regards it), complimenting (or insulting) him, his challengers, and his readers. As a result of this practice, I have felt no hesitation in carrying on researches of my own into the question of precisely what lay behind the religious puzzles expressed by the Bishop and others like him—the question that MacIntyre tried to answer by recourse to socio-psychology and that the newspapers had no sooner touched than they abandoned it.

At the time of publication of the "Debate," I was living in New York, and if the Bishop and his star witnesses were scattered widely over two continents, the eminent American theologian Reinhold Niebuhr was only a few minutes away by taxi. I decided to look him up, and telephoned him at his home. A woman's voice said she would put her husband on the wire.

"By afternoon I'm very tired, but I can see you late in the morning," Niebuhr said, in a middle-western voice. He explained that he had been quite ill.

I was admitted to the Niebuhrs' apartment, on the fifth floor of a building on upper Riverside Drive, by Mrs. Niebuhr. She showed me into her husband's study, a comfortably furnished room, in which Niebuhr was sitting at his desk using an electric typewriter. Niebuhr, a large man of seventy-three, was dressed in a loose-fitting light-blue suit and a plain red tie. He slowly stood up and gave me a firm handshake. "You must have known from talking to my wife on the phone that she's English," he said, with a laugh. "As soon as she says, 'Ursula here,' everyone knows that she's English."

"I could be Australian," Mrs. Niebuhr said, and, indicating an easy chair next to the desk, she added, "I think you'll be comfy there. I've had the twin chair of this in my office at Barnard. I was the head of the Religion Department there." A poodle bounced in, and Mrs. Niebuhr patted him. "He's called Jonathan. He's named after Jonathan Bingham," she said.

"Jonathan Edwards, darling," Niebuhr said.

"Well, he's named after *several* Jonathans," Mrs. Niebuhr said. "He *looks* like Jonathan Bingham, but he was named after Jonathan Edwards because he was born in Stockbridge, up in the Berkshires, where we now have a country house. We also thought of naming him Nathaniel Hawthorne, since Hawthorne lived in Stockbridge, too."

Mrs. Niebuhr then said she would make some coffee, and left the room.

I asked Niebuhr what he thought of "Honest to God."

"I'm not much in touch with English thought," he said. "I've been on the shelf since Archbishop Temple. But I was quite surprised that the Bishop of Woolwich should come on the ideas of Bultmann and Tillich so late. I mean, he's a New Testament scholar, and he should have known long ago what Bultmann and Tillich had been saying—that religious statements are symbolic, and that all religious statements are mythological. Many people have been saying this kind of thing about the New Testament for years." Niebuhr talked haltingly, but his voice carried, as though he were used to speaking in a lecture hall, without a microphone. "There are very few theologians today who believe the Resurrection actually happened," he went on. "There is a progressive retrogression in the New Testament. I mean, there are more and more physical details about Christ's appearance, but the Bishop seems to have just come upon the ideas of Bultmann and Tillich. He did, however, succeed in popularizing those ideas, though I don't think he quite got Tillich right."

I asked if he would explain.

"Well, Tillich has this Neoplatonic side to him, a mystical side," Niebuhr said. (Tillich was still living at the time.) "He's very otherworldly in his morality. I mean, I'm not a theologian," he said, even though he was the author of the major theological work "The Nature and Destiny of Man." "I've spent my life in ethics, in social ethics, in theological education. Tillich is a theologian. He's the most learned man I know. Morality has always been an issue with us. We've been debating it ever since he came to this country. I heard him preach a sermon once on that very difficult passage in the Bible, 'Unto every one that hath shall be given, and he shall have abundance; but from him that hath not shall be taken away even that which he hath.' He said this was a comment on the injustice in the world. He said there was no justice in the world except as it was grounded in God. You see, he removed himself from all the moral issues that have always occupied me. This is his otherworldliness. Robinson didn't touch on this. Tillich dedicated one of his books—'Morality and Beyond'—to me. Doing that was a scandal. I was embarrassed by the dedication, since morality has always been a point with us. But we were both social radicals, and we both thought that the world depression and the Second World War were going to end the bourgeois order. After the war, Tillich went to the Metropolitan Opera and he came back and told me that he had just witnessed a very *symbolic* thing: there were all these upper bourgeois in their box seats who didn't know yet that their culture was finished. He tends to see everything symbolically."

"The difference between you and Tillich, darling, is that he has a system and you have none," Mrs. Niebuhr said, coming in with coffee. She had put on a raincoat. "He's like a snail who has a shell or house over him that he's spun out. What is the German word for that?"

"Why have you put on a raincoat?" Niebuhr asked.

"Because I'm taking Jonathan out for a short walk," Mrs. Niebuhr said.

"A lot of people were surprised that a bishop would speak out as Robinson did," Niebuhr continued when Mrs. Niebuhr had left. "Churchmen are always at the tail end of any intellectual movement. In Germany, there is a complete separation between the theological thinking in the universities and the theological thinking in the church. Karl Barth has now become a pillar of orthodoxy, and in the universities they have moved on from Barth and now study Bultmann. Like Tillich and Bultmann, Karl Barth started out being a creative theologian. His book 'The Epistle to the Romans,' which came out in 1918, was very creative. But later, with 'Church Dogmatics,' he became very orthodox. I've always said that it took a century for Lutheranism to become orthodoxy. Sixteenth-century Lutherans were radical, seventeenth-century Lutherans were arch-orthodox. But Barth became orthodox within the space of a few years."

It was clear that it was a considerable effort for Niebuhr to talk, and that he was getting tired, so a few minutes later I took my leave.

Such books of Tillich's as I had looked at or been able to read through were difficult to assess. There was, for instance, his three-volume magnum opus, the first volume of which appeared in 1951, and which grouped systematically all the ideas on theology that he had developed over half a century. Yet these synoptic tomes, called flatly "Systematic Theology," were written, I thought, from a point of view that was, in a sense, so out of step with the twentieth century (the tone as well as the sweeping nature of the undertaking was distinctly Germanic and nineteenth-century) that the construct as a whole tended, in spite of brilliant individual insights, to distort whatever it encompassed. Moreover, the systematic treatment almost committed the reader to accept all the connected ideas as an entity, and the chances of any contemporary student's doing this could be judged from a passage, central to Tillich's *Weltanschauung,* that was headed "The Kingdom of God and the Ambiguities of Historical Self-Integration":

We have described the ambiguities of history as consequences of the ambiguities of life processes in general. The self-integration of life under the dimension of history shows the ambiguities implied in the drive toward centeredness: the ambiguities of "empire" and of "control," the first appearing in the drive of expansion toward a universal historical unity, and the second, in the drive toward a centered unity in the particular history-bearing group. In each case the ambiguity of power lies behind the ambiguities of historical integration. So the question arises: What is the relation of the Kingdom of God to the ambiguities of power? The answer to this question is also the answer to the question of the relation of the churches to power. The basic theological answer must be that, since God as *the* power of being is the source of all particular powers of being, power is divine in its essential nature. The symbols of power for God or the Christ or the church in biblical literature are abundant. And Spirit is the dynamic unity of power and meaning. The depreciation of power in most pacifist pronouncements is unbiblical as well as unrealistic. Power is the eternal possibility of resisting non-being. God and the Kingdom of God "exercise" this power eternally. But in the divine life—of which the divine kingdom is the creative self-manifestation—the ambiguities of power, empire, and control are conquered by unambiguous life.

One felt that even those stalwarts who were prepared to cast their ballots for the program might hesitate before Tillich's language, for his works, though composed in English, read like literal translations of German and, in addition, had been subjected to the influence of various editors and assistants and secretaries who had helped him with each volume. It was hardly surprising that even crucial terms should shift from upper to lower case, putting one in mind of Don Marquis's archy, and that the sources, instead of being listed in footnotes, should be squeezed into the text: "If one followed the principle that, under certain conditions, quantity becomes quality (Hegel), one would be justified in distinguishing the dimensions of the subatomic, of the astronomical, and of that between them which appears in the ordinary human encounter with reality." The more or less complementary volumes of sermons, "The Eternal Now," "The New Being," and "The Shaking of the Foundations," which were written for a much larger constituency of readers, used some of the central terms and concepts of "Systematic Theology" yet achieved at times an almost mystical power. Yet in the cold light of reason the sermons presented the same philosophical difficulties. Nor was Tillich unaware of these problems. In an intellectual autobiography printed in a commemorative volume entitled "The Theology of Paul Tillich," he noted, "I once said to a Logical Positivist that I would like him to attend my lectures and to raise his finger if something is said that lacks rationality. He answered that he could not accept this task because he would have to raise his finger during the whole lecture." Tillich, however, seemed to be beyond perturbation. In the same essay that contained this anecdote were a number of sanguine passages, among them "For many years I have avoided the term 'absolute' with reference to God. 'Unconditional' means that the realm of finitude is transcended, 'absolute' excludes finitude from a static infinite, a position which I, like Mr. Hartshorne, reject. In such cases precision is not the problem, but conceptual implications."

Yet Jerald Brauer, dean of the University of Chicago Divinity School, where Tillich was then a professor, instead of regarding Tillich as a voice from the past, felt sure that he was a man who spoke to the future. Brauer explained this view to me by saying, "You see, all his life he has been speaking to the people on the borderline of religion, people who were outside the church but leaning toward it, but *now* the people who are in the church, even those of us in theology, find *ourselves* to be also on the borderline of religion. The people who are on the borderline are growing in number everywhere. They are the people for whom Tillich's theology is really made, so Tillich now has more to say than ever." Indeed, in the opinion of many people, Tillich stood astride the dominions of theology like a colossus, or, as Dr. John Bennett, president of Union Theological Seminary, has put it, "a cathedral—one has to walk around him to see him." In fact, except for Emil Brunner, of Zurich, and perhaps Reinhold Niebuhr, Tillich's only peers were considered to be Barth and Bultmann. Langdon Gilkey, a professor of theology at the University of Chicago Divinity School, who had explored the connections among these titans, told me that one of the reasons for their eminence was that they had buried the liberal theology of the late nineteenth century, which is remembered today mostly for its overly optimistic view of man and its uncritical acceptance of the bourgeois order. Barth and Bultmann are now in their eighties, and Tillich was seventy-nine when he died, and they had all passed into surveys of contemporary theology as "the neo-orthodox" (their repudiation of their elders had flung them back into the classical, or orthodox, way of speaking about God), yet no one who had come along since could begin to match their achievements or their influence. But Gilkey had written, in a paper:

> . . . The older neo-orthodox leaders had unwittingly "pushed God out of ordinary existence" to its edge (Bultmann), to its depths (Tillich), or to the special place where secular existence had been entered and transformed by revelation (Barth). In the thought of each, secular existence as it is *ordinarily* lived and understood was seen to be devoid of the divine and so in turn the divine could only be found in these special "unsecular" places, dimensions, or depths. Ironically, therefore, neo-orthodoxy did in theory what its oldest and deadliest antagonist, the Enlightenment, had long since done in practice, namely, removed God from the ordinary structures of normal life. So long as a lively sense of the reality and ultimate significance of these special places, of that divine boundary, of that holy depth, or of that sacred Word remained, as they surely did in neo-orthodox theology, total secularism was, so to speak, held at bay. With Bonhoeffer, however, the theological significance of these special divine dimensions and places disappears with the basic repudiation of dependence on God; instead of the means of grace, they become the empty "religion" that separates man from ordinary life and that is thus alien to "real Christianity."

On Friday, October 22, 1965, Tillich died in the University of Chicago's Billings Hospital, where he had been admitted the previous week after a heart attack. A short while before, I had the good fortune to meet him. I saw him one afternoon at the University of Chicago, in his office, which was on the fourth floor of Swift Hall—a building that Frank Lloyd Wright would have described as "cast-iron Gothic." The office, a cubicle without so much as a picture (its total contents were a bookcase, a sofa, a desk, two straight-backed chairs, an electric coffeemaker, a pot of chrysanthemums, and a blue beret and an overcoat hanging from a peg), was a part of a suite, which included a larger outer office that was occupied by his secretary, a classroom, and a couple of other faculty offices. Tillich turned out to be a rather patriarchal figure with abundant white hair and dressed in a noticeably new blue suit. He greeted me quietly, waved me to one of the straight chairs, and then went over to his desk and sat down.

His secretary brought in the afternoon mail.

Tillich started looking through the letters, mumbling, almost to himself, "I have so many pressures on me. If you only knew the pressures! My letters have been growing each year—sometimes there are twenty-five or thirty a day. I reply to all of them. I use this office and my secretary only for writing letters. I've never been capable of not answering letters. It's the *agape* in me. If I had been born in Tibet, I would have retired twenty years ago. It would not have been my role to answer letters." He pushed the letters aside and said, "I have recently had troubles with my health, and my doctor has told me to lie down—especially after a meal. Do you mind if I talk lying down?"

I said of course I didn't, and Tillich walked over to the sofa, which was opposite his desk. He sat, stood, and walked very straight. He had on plastic-rimmed glasses, which were rather too small for him and tended to ride up his nose. Having adjusted them, he stretched out. Just then, the telephone rang in the outer office. Tillich got up quickly and went over to his desk. (Dean Brauer had told me that Tillich never let a secretary answer his telephone. According to Brauer, this was open to two interpretations: that he didn't trust anybody, and—Brauer's own interpretation—that he didn't want a third presence to come between him and another person. Brauer had gone on to say, "This is typical of him. He's the most democratic German professor there ever was. When I first met him, I was hired to be his assistant at Union. I walked into his office in fear and trembling. He was reading at his desk by a very small light. He looked up and said, 'What may I do for you?' I told him I had been hired as his assistant. He asked my name. I answered, 'Brauer.' He asked, 'But what's your name?' I repeated, 'Brauer.' Then he said, 'No, what is your *name?* What people call you by?' I replied, 'Jerald'—of course, no one ever called me that, they all called me Jerry—and then he said, 'Jerry, call me Paulus.' ")

Tillich picked up the telephone and said, "This is Professor Tillich. . . . No, you've got the wrong number." He hung up.

Thinking that I'd better get to the subject of my interest as quickly as possible, I asked him a general question about his ideas.

"My work is an infinite subject," he said. "Ask me some specific, finite questions."

Upon hearing the words "infinite" and "finite," though I do not have much in common with the Logical Positivists, I mentally raised my finger, but aloud I said that, through Robinson, some of his ideas had become very well known both in England and in America. He nodded, lay down on the sofa again, and said, "I've never had much influence in England. The English are not worried by the problems of loneliness, despair—are not touched by the whole existential movement. I came in on the peak of the wave of 'Honest to God,' and will probably go out when the wave breaks."

I told him Dean Brauer had said of him that he spoke to people on the borderline of religion and that his ideas would have increasing relevance in the future.

"I think my influence is already felt all over the world through my books—except for England," he said. "More than twelve of my books have been translated into Japanese. About four years ago, I was in Japan, and I talked to a lot of Buddhist scholars and monks. I found that they had heard of me, and one of them even admitted that reincarnation in Buddhism was a symbolic statement, as I had thought it was."

I had encountered in many places—including some pages of Tillich—the idea that most religious statements were symbolic and few could be taken as literally true, I said, and yet it was difficult to see where one was to draw the line between symbolic and literal statements—and, indeed, it seemed that making the distinction at all might open the way to an erosion of religion. It was not easy for me, I told Tillich, to take the matter of the historical Jesus, for instance, as in any sense unimportant for Christianity.

"Symbols are representations," he said. "Bread is something I eat; it's not the body of Christ. It's a symbol of His sacrifice. Grape is something I suck, and wine is something I drink; it isn't the blood of Christ literally. All statements in the New Testament are symbolic in the sense that they are analogues, parables, and we have to interpret them in an existential way. By 'existential way' I mean that people's lives are different at different times, and the Bible has to be reinterpreted each time according to the situation in which people find themselves. A lot of people now go to church for whom the old language and old symbols mean nothing. But there are certain symbols that last, like the king symbol, which is central to the Bible. Christ was the representative of God on earth. He was the son of the king, the ruler, God. He was born and anointed. The king symbol is very old. The Egyptians had a king-god."

I had lately heard a preacher on the radio tell the parable of the sheep and the goats in terms of unions and management, I remarked—a kind of updating of the Gospels that seemed to have become quite common recently. I asked Tillich cautiously, "If one day kings and monarchies were to disappear everywhere, giving place to presidents and constitutions, would the Bible message have to be translated into some new idiom?"

"Even though the symbolic material should change from kings

to presidents—even if there should be no king at some time—I think we would still think of God as a monarch, because there are certain symbolic materials which last," he replied. "Certain symbols do become meaningless. The Holy Virgin is such a meaningless symbol now."

"Is Hell a meaningful or meaningless symbol?" I asked.

"I don't think symbols of damnation and salvation—or immortality—mean anything," he replied. "Any description of an afterlife in Christianity is only an attempt at a description of an eternal state. I know a lot of Christians think that immortality will be like those cemeteries out in California—they'll wake up after death and be in one of those cemeteries. But I can't tell you what there is after death. I think of death only as returning to the eternal, which is out of time and space. I first sensed what this eternal was when I was eight years old and I looked at my father's church—it was fifteenth-century Gothic—and saw the beauty in it. I remember that was my first experience of the eternal. And since then I have been learning something about the eternal by reading and contemplation and discussions such as this one."

The mention of our discussion in such a context made me bold, and I pressed my question about literal versus symbolic statements. I asked Tillich if he would elaborate on his view about the symbolic content of the New Testament.

"I think the Bible ought to be treated like any other literary-historical document," Tillich said. "We ought to find out whether the different parts of the Bible are true or not in the same way we find out whether any other literary-historical document is true or not. The Gospel of John, we know, came about a hundred years after Christ and has a lot of Pauline and post-Pauline theology in it. It is based on earlier reports but itself is not a report, so we treat it differently from the three others. Besides the historical aspect of criticism, there is the literary, the legendary, and the mythological."

I asked Tillich whether, as an example, he thought Christ really performed miracles or whether he thought the miracles were "mythological," in Bultmann's sense.

"I think there is good evidence for some of those healings that He did," he replied equably. "But in history, of course, you never have definite evidence for anything."

But how, I insisted, could symbols change, even lose all meaning, without affecting the content of the Christian message?

"Man is conditioned," Tillich said. "He's conditioned by his birth, by his country, by his experience." He went on to develop this theme in a series of brief statements. As far as I could follow it, he seemed to be saying that the content changed along with the symbol, that both were relative to the age in which they were brought forth and, later, to the age in which they were remembered, and that they were existential in the sense that they were completely conditioned by the existence of the particular circumstances under which they took form, including the individual persons who originally gave expression to them.

This was such a thoroughgoing kind of relativism that I was impelled to ask, "Was there anything about Christ which freed Him from the shackles of His time and situation?"

"Christ *was* conditioned, but He sacrificed Himself, sacrificed His particularity, for something universal, for something unconditional," Tillich replied. "The unconditional is the infinite. The experience of the unconditional is mystical. A lot of people don't like to use the word 'mystical,' but I don't mind it. I think everybody has this emptiness when he doesn't have the experience of the unconditional—he feels this emptiness about him. And whether one has had religious upbringing or not, this feeling of emptiness expresses the need for the unconditional, for religion. There are juvenile delinquents everywhere, so there is great meaninglessness in existence today."

"What about some of the existentialist writers, like Camus,

who say the emptiness and meaninglessness are the natural state
of man?"

"I think that despair in itself is religious," Tillich said. "It
is the ground of one's being. It was the ground of Camus's
being."

Someone who said that he did not believe in anything and
wanted to face up to the fact that there was nothing—if *he*
could be regarded as religious, then, I asked, who could be
called non-religious?

"The ground of one's being is what one feels deeply," Tillich
said benignly. "Despair was a *necessary* condition of Camus's
being, but I don't think it could be a *sufficient* condition of
Camus's being or of anyone's being."

I changed my approach. I asked, "What about people who
don't feel any need for religion, who don't feel this emptiness—
skeptics like Bertrand Russell, say?"

"They deceive themselves," he said. "There are certain people
who just can't see the color green, and one can't argue with
them. Russell would be one of them."

"And supposing they said that you might be deceived in
thinking that people had this need for religion, and that 'unconditional' and 'ground of being' were not very meaningful
terms?"

"On that basis, there could be no argument," he said. "But I
might give them the five classical proofs for the existence of
God, the five arguments for God, which Aquinas gives—they
can be found in any history of philosophy or history of theology
—and then point to this awareness of ultimate reality, the unconditional, in everybody."

I asked Tillich where his views belonged in relation to
Christian theology.

He laughed quietly and, becoming a little more expansive,
said, "You must meet Barth. From him you will get a lot of
personal sympathy for me and also a lot of condemnation. Posi-

tivists say that all statements that cannot be verified—experimentally, scientifically—are meaningless. Barth agrees with them, but he exempts revelation. In doing so, he becomes—in a sense— just as orthodox as a fundamentalist, because the Bible for him remains the word of God. Barth therefore regards me as worse than heretical. He thinks I am not even religious. But what is a heresy? Protestantism itself was a heresy to begin with. From Catholicism's point of view, Protestants were heretics, but now the Catholics call Protestants 'separated brethren.' It's one of the good things about Christianity that it has the power to reform from within. Organized Christianity makes less and less sense in the increasingly secular world. We are now living in a mass culture, and to people formed by mass media and secular interests traditional religion has no meaning. I was a chaplain in the German Army in the First World War. If I used Biblical language to the soldiers, it meant nothing to them—they were about to die, and yet the Bible had nothing to say to them. I preached sermons, therefore, that never used any of the language of the Bible. They were a little mystical, a little poetical, and also had a touch of common sense, and they had an effect. I think that in the secular world churches must find a new function, they must take on new meaning. If there is no religion of any kind, the void is filled by quasi-religion, whether it's science or Fascism."

"And how would you distinguish true from false gods?"

"Quasi-religion is taking something limited and making it into the ultimate. Fascism raised something limited to the ultimate. That was quasi-religion. Hitler was a demonic force, and whenever there are such demonic forces, anti-demonic forces come into being. I face this problem in a volume of my 'Systematic Theology.' History is the clash of the demon and the anti-demon. Catholicism had become demonic, so it brought forth Protestantism. Even the Pope now is demonic, I think. Many of my Catholic friends are beginning to see that now, but they haven't said it yet. He should be just a symbol, but anybody who raises something limited to the ultimate—that's demonic."

I asked, "What, actually, is this ultimate?"

"It's the utimate concern, the infinite, the ground of one's being," he said. "The depth of one's experience, the awareness of the holy. At some moments when I am listening to Mozart or looking at a painting, I think that I see the holy, that I know what's holy. Buddha was a representation of the holy, and Christ was a representation of the holy, and it's this experience of the holy that is the important thing. If some people claim to be holy and are not, and do no harm, that's perfectly all right. But if they are dangerous, then there has to be anti-demonization. People live in different circumstances and in different societies, and different religions are meaningful to them. But there are primitive religions that are all superstition and magic. I think in some cases conversion is justified, especially in the case of primitive, superstitious religions. But as for the higher religions—there are about six, seven of them, and they have been here for thousands of years—they may have some superstitious element in them which we must demythologize, but nevertheless they have the concern for the ultimate, and this is what I call the ground of being. Because of my upbringing and culture, I just don't understand the religious representations of the other higher religions; because of my upbringing and culture, I think Christianity is the best religion. Religion is a balance of freedom and destiny. Destiny is the historical situation, the conditions such as where one was born and where one lives. It's a problem I face in a volume of my 'Systematic Theology.' Religion is not a matter of decision or choice. In the first place, it's a matter of destiny. The freedom, the decision, comes in only when the destiny is changed somewhat. Then a decision can modify the destiny."

Several fingers had gone up inside my head, but I did not

wish to add to the pressures that Tillich was under. He forced himself up off the couch and into his desk chair, and, rather absently, answered a few more questions—these about himself.

He told me that in 1924 he had married Hannah Werner, who had never had any predominant interest in Christian theology but, instead, was inclined to Eastern thought—she had read the Book of the Dead—and, lately, to Buddhism in particular. They had come to America in 1933, when Tillich was put on Hitler's list of proscribed professors. Richard Niebuhr, Reinhold Niebuhr's brother, had translated one of his books, and Reinhold Niebuhr, the moment he read a newspaper account of Tillich's expulsion, had invited him to come to Union Theological Seminary. Until he came to America and learned English, his education had been mainly in Latin and Greek. Along with a happy academic career, he and Mrs. Tillich had had a very active social life until the past year, when it had been curtailed a little because of his health. Wherever they had happened to be, they had generally attended a cocktail party every evening and arranged either to dine out with friends or to have friends in for dinner. Their friendships had always cut across all departments of a university. In addition to close friends, he had other friends, scattered all the way from San Francisco to Boston, Göttingen, and Hamburg, many of whom he had met in passing or had only corresponded with. In these and other centers, groups regularly met in homes and clubs to study his works and propagate his ideas. Those of his followers who were in Chicago might see the Tillichs at home in their apartment, in the Windermere Hotel, overlooking a museum and Lake Michigan. Because the Tillichs did not stay in any one place for very long—they were leaving the next day for the Santa Barbara branch of the University of California, where they spent a couple of months each winter—they preferred living in hotels, though they owned a house in East Hampton, which contained such of Tillich's books as he had not already donated to Harvard. They liked spending their summers in East Hampton, for Tillich felt at one with nature there. The house was not far from the ocean, which for him represented infinity, and surrounding the house were two and a half acres of land that he called "the park." Part of it was allowed to grow wild except for a narrow path, which he used for daily walks, and if he passed an interesting tree or shrub or flower, he would break off any conversation he might be carrying on in order to scrutinize the mystery and beauty of nature.

If Tillich had endeavored to do what Walter Kaufmann might call a "gerrymandering" of God—to reconstitute God in order to find a place for Him in an increasingly secular world— there were other theologians, it appeared, who, perhaps taking their cue from such arguments of modern philosophy as that there was no evidence for the existence of God but, in the evil in the world, plenty of evidence for the opposite view, and from such Biblical passages as "Then came Jesus forth, wearing the crown of thorns, and the purple robe. And Pilate saith unto them, Behold the man! [*Ecce homo!*]," had eliminated God altogether, though they still called themselves Christians. In the "Debate," Robinson had referred to one of these avant-garde theologians: "Whether, or in what sense, the Gospel can be given expression without recourse to metaphysical statements I do not know. . . . Professor Paul van Buren, [in] 'The Secular Meaning of the Gospel' . . . clearly believes that the Christian who takes his secularity seriously can and must abjure metaphysics, though he quotes Professor Ian Ramsey, on whose position he builds, as defending the term." Without pausing over this inconsistency, the Bishop had charged ahead: "Van Buren's book I regard as one of the most exciting and disturbing I have read. It is a sustained attempt to answer the question, 'How may a Christian who is himself a secular man understand the Gospel in a secular way?' A brilliantly original thesis and something of a theological tour de force, it seeks to do justice to an orthodox Christology based on Barth and Bonhoeffer at the same time as taking the philosophical critique of Wittgenstein and the linguistic analysts with equal seriousness. I believe it is a major contribution and may already bear out my conviction that in retrospect 'Honest to God' 'will be seen to have erred in not being nearly radical enough.' "

The Bishop's comparison of his book with that of van Buren —an American Episcopal clergyman who teaches at Temple University, in Philadelphia—surprised me. In "The Secular Meaning of the Gospel," van Buren argued that, as secular men, we could and must present the Christian message without using the language of metaphysics or the term "God." He would cast out both the transcendental and the supernatural elements from Christianity, and build faith not on God but on the empirical personality of Jesus Christ as we know Him from the Gospels and from His influence on His disciples and, through them, on people down the ages. As a quartet of distinguished philosophers and theologians who had discussed "The Secular Meaning of the Gospel" on the Third Programme, in London, in September, 1964, saw it, the main objection to this thesis was that if the Bishop and his mentors had banished God in favor of Christ, then van Buren, perhaps without realizing it, had gone a step further and banished Christ in favor of His disciples. In the words of one critic on the panel, "He seems to me to be saying sometimes, 'You can register how striking and amazing a man Jesus was by His effect on His disciples;' he's also saying, 'This effect on the disciples has to be taken terribly seriously as a paradigm of moral life and the foundation of one's outlook, because it was a reaction to such an extraordinary man.' Now this seems to me to be just going round in a hopeless circle. It's just putting all your faith really in the apostles rather than on Jesus." Actually, a glance at van Buren's book showed that though he seemed to be new to the ways of modern philosophy—

he tended to lump all the disparate Oxford philosophers together as "linguistic analysts"—such philosophy as he had at his
command had nevertheless led him to push on to conclusions
that the Bishop and his mentors had shrunk from, so that
Robinson's praise for van Buren made one think that the
Bishop, after "Honest to God," felt the need to take under his
protective wing, and cassock, all comers (a hunch confirmed by
his more recent support of another far-out book, Harvey Cox's
"The Secular City," of which he writes, "Is secularization the
enemy of the Gospel or the fruit of the Gospel? Here is a
major contribution by a brilliant young theologian, of whom we
shall undoubtedly be hearing more").

Van Buren is a member of the group called the Christian
Radicals—a group so much discussed in England and America
that Langdon Gilkey had gone as far as to try to compile a book
of essays on them. A draft of Gilkey's introduction to the
projected volume, tracing the origins of the movement and
setting forth what he considered its sweeping program, had
been circulating for some time among prospective contributors,
which included the Christian Radicals themselves. Whatever
merits such a book might have—and some of the theologians
whom Gilkey approached thought the movement ephemeral and
beneath notice and, in any case, limited to only three men,
William Hamilton, Thomas J. J. Altizer, and van Buren (interestingly, Gabriel Vahanian, of Syracuse University, whose
book "Death of God" Bultmann regards as one of the most
exciting he has read in recent years, was not included, because
he was considered to be too conservative)—reading Gilkey's
paper left me in no doubt that he considered the Christian
Radicals a major challenge to theology:

In proclaiming the death of God, or at least of all language about
Him, the new theology makes the most fundamental possible break
with the long tradition of Christian theological discourse. . . . By asserting the death of God and the need to construct a theology with-

out Him, it issues a fundamental challenge to the essential structure
of Biblical and Christian thought not only, of course, about God, but
also about Jesus, nature, history and mankind—and for this reason,
if for no other, it must be comprehended and answered. . . . At least
it is ironically true that Chicago is now regarded as jointly defending
with Union and Yale the "establishment" in theology; and the reason
is that membership in this conservative establishment is determined
by the mere continuing use of God-language rather than by a static
devotion to traditional or orthodox modes of theology.

Gilkey continues:

From Barth this movement has accepted the radical separation of
the divine and the secular, of God and ordinary experience, and so
of theological language and philosophy; and it approves his further
separation of Christianity and religion, and the consequent centering
of all theological and religious concerns, not on any innate "religiousness," "religious a priori," or religious "depths," but solely on Jesus
Christ. From Tillich it has accepted the campaign against theism,
and against personalistic and mythological language about God. From
Bultmann it has absorbed the polemic against ancient "mythical"
categories in theology, which polemic needed only to be enlarged to
include biblical-kerygmatic as well as objective-interventionist theological language about God to become very radical indeed. . . . Apparently this generation finds itself influenced solely by these particular *negative* elements of the older theology and not at all by the
balancing positive elements in each case: the emphasis on God, revelation, and the Word in Barth; on an ontological analysis of existential
"depth," on revelation, and so on Being Itself in Tillich; and on
existential inwardness and self-understanding "at the boundary" and
"before God" in Bultmann. If these negative elements in neo-
orthodoxy alone are stressed, there is solely in that inheritance itself
substantial ground for a radical revolution.

When I heard that van Buren, along with his intellectual ship-
mate William Hamilton, who is a professor of theology at Col-
gate Rochester Divinity School, was coming to New York to

attend a conference at Union Theological Seminary, I decided
to look both men up. In the hope that Hamilton might give
me a gentle introduction to van Buren's ideas, I talked with him
first. I knew something about Hamilton's own thought from a
thinly disguised autobiographical article he had written for
Theology Today, entitled "Thursday's Child: The Theologian
Between Today and Tomorrow." It had complained about the
difficulties of being a theologian in modern times:

> The theologian is sometimes inclined to suspect that Jesus Christ
> is best understood not as either the object or ground of faith, and
> not as person, event, or community, but simply as a place to be, a
> standpoint. That place is, of course, alongside the neighbor, being
> for him. This may be the meaning of Jesus' true humanity and it
> may even be the meaning of his divinity, and thus of divinity itself.
> In any case, now—even when he knows so little about what to be-
> lieve—he does know where to be. Today, for example, he is with
> the colored community in its struggle. . . . He has been drawn, then,
> to these worldly places by love (not by apologetics or evangelism),
> and it is his hope that in such places his faithlessness and dishonesty
> may be broken. His love is not a secure and confident one, and thus
> it is not condescending. It is not, therefore, what some men call
> *agape.* It is a broken love, one that is needy and weak. It is thus a
> little like what men call *eros.*

I looked to Hamilton's conversation to make his meaning clear
and, upon meeting him, immediately asked him where he belonged in relation to traditional Christianity.

His reply was "I am still in the space between the ins and
the outs as far as traditional Christianity is concerned. Half my
day is spent praying or preaching, and I find no trouble in
writing or saying prayers, though they are mostly about my
inability to pray. I still teach seminary students who are going to
be pastors, though I have had to explain my writings to the
president of the seminary and to my colleagues. I don't think
that van Buren faces some of my problems. At Temple, the

chairman of the Religion Department is a Buddhist, so van
Buren doesn't face my problem of being in or out of the Establishment. If I become an out, I will start teaching college undergraduates, and give up teaching seminary students. There are a
lot of people teaching in the religion departments of colleges
who do not believe in God—it's not a problem. But with seminary students— If I do become an out, perhaps I will just move
over to the University of Rochester full time, as there is a lot
of intellectual bohemianism among the undergraduates there. I
think a lot of people nowadays *make* it without believing in God,
and without despairing about not believing in God, so God
may be dead or gone. I mean the Judaeo-Christian God. But I
am still waiting and hoping for God to rise up again. *But* I am
beginning to feel that the time has come for me to put up or shut
up, for me to be an in or an out."

I arranged to meet van Buren one afternoon at a French
restaurant on the West Side. When I arrived, I found him seated
at a table in the back of the nearly empty room. Van Buren,
who was educated at St. Paul's and Harvard, at the Episcopal
Theological School in Cambridge, and in Basel, Switzerland,
where he had studied with Barth, was only forty and looked
even younger. He had brown hair and hazel eyes, and he had
brought along a pipe.

I pulled a chair up to the table, and, after a bit of small talk,
asked, "How do you think your views compare with those
of Robinson?"

"I subscribe wholeheartedly to the first couple of chapters of
'Honest to God,'" he said. "That is, up until he gets onto the
ground of our being. Those chapters are sort of his survey of
what has happened in the West, which has made the whole
language and thought form of traditional Christianity—God 'up
there' and 'out there'—problematical. Yes, those pages could
have been an introduction to my own book, 'The Secular Meaning of the Gospel.' I thought as I read them: Isn't it delightful

that somebody else is writing about this, too! But the Tillichian line of thinking on which Robinson leaned so heavily farther on in the book I found very foreign to the world in which I live. I found it positing an ideal realm that, it seems to me, is neither called for nor necessary."

"How did you feel about the rest of the book—the pages that come after the discussion of the ground of being?" I asked.

"I think that if the Christology chapter had been written first and he had paid more attention to the problem of language, then he wouldn't have had to write the ground-of-our-being chapter at all."

"Even if Robinson had organized his book differently, wouldn't there still have been a disagreement between you?" I asked. "You criticize him for keeping God in some form, but he feels that you leave out God altogether."

"Yes, Robinson's main criticism of me is that I've said the problem is not so much that the traditional God has died as that the very *word* 'God' has died. And he feels that we cannot finally get along without in some way using the word 'God.' What I'm thinking now is a lot more radical even than what I said in my book. A couple of years have gone by since I finished writing it. Yes, Robinson has a very conservative streak. He has been caught in the middle on this whole thing about God, and he admits that. On the one hand, he responds to all radical voices, and, on the other hand, can say—on top of that, he can say—'I am deeply concerned that God be known.' All this thing about the ground of our being is simply an attempt to make a kind of sense out of the traditional language about God. Fundamentally, he says, there's the same thing to be talked about, and we must just find a new way of doing it. The trouble with Robinson and Tillich is the way they use 'being.' Their use of the word rests on a misunderstanding of the logic of how we use the verb 'to be,' because 'being' is not a predicate, it is not a characteristic, it is not a quality that things have in addition to other things we can say about them, and to look for being or the ground of our being behind all that is can be compared to looking for Oxford University behind the various colleges, professors, lecturers, students, buildings, and so on that make up what we call the university."

Van Buren's criticism of "being," in particular, and of Tillichian terminology, in general, I recognized as fairly standard. More interesting was his remark that he had lately gone even further than he had gone in "The Secular Meaning of the Gospel," so I turned next to his radicalism and asked, "What is a Christian Radical?"

"Well, in America, there is supposed to be Altizer, of Emory University, and there is Bill Hamilton, and then there's me. Langdon Gilkey says that we are the Radicals, and I suppose we are. But Altizer and I have never met, and Bill Hamilton and I met for the first time only in 1964."

I asked him what, exactly, he thought was radical about the three of them.

"Well, Langdon Gilkey says we belong to a 'God is dead' movement, but I think Altizer and Bill Hamilton and I are saying different things. If I understand Bill correctly, the feeling I get from him is that God is on vacation, so we have to get along without God. But I can't decide whether Bill means that God is absent in a historical or a poetical sense. I suppose he is taking after Bonhoeffer and his idea that man has come of age, that God Himself has decided that man doesn't need Him any longer, and Bill is saying this is the time for the man of faith to exercise patience. Sometimes Bill gives the impression of someone waiting for faith, and at other times he says that man is without faith or hope. But the element of waiting, it seems to me, involves in some sense faith and in some sense hope. So you may raise the question of whether faith is possible at all without God. Altizer—I have only read a couple of his articles. As far as I understand *him*, he believes in the God of the Judgment Day, he accepts the eschatology of the Bible. Altizer wants to draw a distinction between the God who is somehow the eschatological God of the Bible, the God of the end (he uses that expression several times in one of his articles: 'God of the end'), who is not so much to be thought of as being behind the scenes ruling over us as somehow there at the end of it all—he draws a distinction between that God and the idea of God that the Christian theologians have developed over the centuries. Yes, he believes in the God of Christian eschatology but not in the *idea* of the God of the theologians, and that— that idea of God—is what has died. Altizer says there can be no theology that does not begin with the death of the God idea."

"But how can you separate the God of the Bible from the God of theology?" I asked, picking one question out of many that occurred to me.

"This is the same argument that goes through my mind: How does the God of the end escape the death that is supposed to come to the idea of God? I don't understand this, you see. My own view on the death of God is that in the last three hundred years or so God as an absolute has dissolved. I don't think that God is just on vacation, or that the Bible God is relevant to anything—"

"What would you like?" The interruption came from a waitress who had been hovering near our table for some time.

"I'd like a beer," van Buren said.

"What kind? Heineken's? Carlsberg? Schlitz? Rheingold?"

"Rheingold, please."

After the waitress had left us, he resumed, "In the whole development of Christianity, God has been, it seems to me, conceived as the absolute, and it seems to me that this whole manner of speaking about the category of the absolute—this has dissolved. Yes, I could put it this way: It's not so much that the classical arguments for the existence of God are wrong, or that we don't follow the arguments and find them convincing, as that the *question* to which the classical proofs were the answer is not a question we would today take to be properly phrased. On this I think Altizer, Hamilton, and I would all agree."

"Are there any other similarities among the three of you?" I asked.

"I can speak up better for similarities between Hamilton and me than I can in respect to Altizer, because I know less about Altizer—he has written less. The similarity between Bill and me lies in our background—a background of study in Biblical theology, and therefore, broadly speaking, an interest in the historical, the human, the realm of the ethical."

"The realm of the ethical?"

"Yes. Of man making his decisions and being responsible for them. If you took me at the stage at which I wrote 'The Secular Meaning of the Gospel,' what took the *place* of theology in the proper sense at that time, for both Hamilton and me, was Christology; that is, a very pronounced emphasis on Jesus of Nazareth. Jesus as the paradigm, I think I would have put it—as the paradigm or model of what human life is. What human life ought to be. A kind of norm in one's understanding of man and human life. Let me say this around one example. One of the ways in which the New Testament writers speak about Jesus is in divine and quasi-divine terms—Son of God, and what have you. All right. My interest is in seeing how these terms function, what they accomplish, what difference it makes whether one denies these terms or subscribes to them, and what difference *this* would make to the pattern of life advocated by the New Testament writers. What I'm trying to do is to understand the Bible on a naturalistic or humanistic level, to find out how the references to the absolute and the supernatural are used in expressing on a human level the understanding and convictions that the New Testament writers had about their world. For by using these large cosmological terms in speaking about this particular happening, this event—the history of Jesus—they were saying the most that they could say about this man. If a man in the first century had wanted to say of a certain person that he had given him an insight into what human life was all about, he would have almost normally said, 'That man is divine.'"

In reading about van Buren—and, indeed, in reading his book, and even talking to him—I had been repeatedly nagged by two personal questions about him: How could a man who had studied with Barth (and Pope John XXIII had once compared Barth's achievement to that of Aquinas) have wandered so far away from his teacher? And, given the fact that he had, how could he go on wearing the collar of a clergyman? Van Buren had given me the impression during our conversation that he could answer questions quite dispassionately, so I now felt no hesitation in putting these to him point-blank. His response was characteristically straightforward.

"Barth says that we have made a fundamental mistake, all of us—my generation, Bonhoeffer's generation—in shifting our attention to man and man's ways of understanding, and the patterns of contemporary thought and all that sort of thing. Barth doesn't think that Bonhoeffer's 'Letters and Papers from Prison' are even worth considering. He thinks they're adolescent. Yes, Barth thinks we have the Word of God in revelations, and then we have the word of the Church, and the job of the theologian is to see how far the two correspond. Barth's volumes and volumes of the 'Church Dogmatics' tried to do this. I sent him a précis of 'The Secular Meaning of the Gospel,' and he thought I had betrayed him. He thinks the job of his students should be to go on revising those 'Dogmatics'—make them more and more nearly perfect. He does not mean this to be an insult to his students; it's just that he thinks of his 'Dogmatics' as very tentative. I think the reason for Bonhoeffer's influence on people my age has to do with his coming at a particular moment. Langdon considers himself a generation older than I am, though

I imagine he is only in his late forties, and he divides his generation from mine—there is some sense to this—according to the
time at which we got interested in theology, whether before the
Second World War or after. When Bonhoeffer's 'Letters and
Papers from Prison' came out, in the early fifties, they were just
the kind of thing my generation was looking for—*I* have read
Bonhoeffer's 'Letters and Papers' again and again—but Langdon
and others weren't so much affected by Bonhoeffer, because they
had got interested in theology before the war. I don't think our
kind of postwar radicalism, the kind of thinking based on Bonhoeffer, is isolated. I think a lot of people are engaged in it, and
Langdon says that, too—that this is a general movement. And
about my being a clergyman—well, I don't pray. I just reflect
on these things. I am ordained, but when I am asked to preach
or to perform services, I usually say I would rather not. I would
ask to be defrocked if that could be done in a quiet, inoffensive
way, but it can't be. Defrocking requires a lot of fuss. The news
of the event would have to be published, and there are a number of Christians—people who believe that the kind of thing
I am doing is making Christianity more meaningful for them—
who would be upset. I don't want to upset them. If I really
thought ordination was so important, or if some authority in
the Episcopal Church came up to me and said that the kind of
thing I was doing was heretical, I would immediately ask to
be defrocked, without a heresy trial or that sort of thing. But
no one has, and the Anglican Church has a tradition of having
some weirdies in it—there have been some pretty freethinking
people in it in the past."

"But do you feel comfortable about calling yourself a Christian?" I asked.

"If some Church authority came up to me and said I wasn't,
I would say that I was perfectly willing to respect the decisions
that the official Christian body wanted to make about what it
would accept and what it would not accept. I wouldn't want to

make an issue of that. I am trying to raise a more important issue: whether or not Christianity is fundamentally about God or about man. That is, putting it rather sharply, I am trying to argue that it *is* fundamentally about man, that its language about God is one way—a dated way, among a number of ways—of saying what it is Christianity wants to say about man and human life and human history. And, if I understand the nature and development of Christology in the history of Christianity, I would want to argue that what Christianity is basically about is a certain form of life—patterns of human existence, norms of human attitudes and dispositions and moral behavior."

"But wouldn't a Christian say that God is indispensable to the form of life you speak of?"

"I wouldn't, because I could prove the same thing from the humanist point of view."

"But why does one need the Christian edifice at all, then?"

"Well, I don't know what is to be gained or lost by calling a particular answer Christian or un-Christian. I would want to say that Christianity, around the figure of Christ—a considerably reinterpreted figure, I would have to admit—has developed a certain image of man and of human relationships. These can also be, and have been, developed in the Western humanistic tradition. Whether and to what extent this humanism was influenced by Christianity is perhaps a secondary question. But if you really got me with my back to the wall, I'd probably want to say I am more concerned about the substance of that Christian picture than about the name by which you call it. If somebody wants to fight about the name, then I guess I would have to admit that I'm just not a Christian."

II

THE EKKLESIA

ONLY in the last few years has theology been taking wide-spread cognizance of the strictures of science, the demands of secularism, and the growing sense of cosmic despair, even though these things have been about, in combination, for several centuries, finding expression during that time in the works of Descartes, Newton, and Laplace, of Schopenhauer, Nietzsche, and Hardy. As change loomed, some philosophers and theologians maintained that theology had been able to keep her counsel for all those centuries merely because of her long-established privileged position, while others contended that she had to ignore outside influences, because the men who talked about God, by definition, could never reach an understanding with the men who talked about science. When the first group of philosophers and theologians went on to declare that the era of ascendancy for theology was at last over—in their view, it had been coming to a close since Copernicus—and that any further delay in the accommodation of theology to the world would condemn the discipline to death by quarantine and by default, the second group argued that, on the contrary, theology was a science in itself, that the word of God, as much of it as was revealed to us, was the same for all time, and that any attempt to revamp the old language and doctrines, however archaic they might appear, would require of theology an alliance so compromising that it would be another form of death. Whatever the rights and wrongs of the opposing views, events today have seemed to favor the group committed to change and adjustment. Not only did Bishop Robinson and Langdon Gilkey think that they had been overtaken by, say, Paul van Buren—who, they were ready to grant, represented something of a movement—but even the late Paul Tillich seemed to feel that he had become vestigial. In the draft of his essay on the so-called Christian Radicals, Gilkey wrote, "This split in theological consciousness just the 'other side of forty' is illustrated in Tillich's remark to me last spring [1964], 'Vy, Langdon, am I so soon on ze dust heap of history?'—and in my answer, 'Don't feel too sorry for yourself—I'm there already too!' "

In my initial reading of "Honest to God," of the criticism of Robinson that appeared in all sections of the British press, and of some other theological works, I had started out by taking it for granted that the Bishop's was a minority view, and probably an avant-garde one. Even though his text was larded with abundant quotations from Tillich, Bultmann, and Bonhoeffer, and his cry was echoed in many quarters, it seemed to me that the Bishop had so neglected the great differences, and resulting tensions, among his sources and had so forced the similarities that what he had presented was a mixture all his own. Also, the New Theology that he and other theologians espoused—the complete merging of Christianity and the secular world, so that an urgent question became, as Bonhoeffer put it for all of them, "In what way are we in a religionless and secular sense Christians, in what way are we the *Ekklesia*, 'those who are called forth,' not conceiving of ourselves religiously as specially favored, but as wholly belonging to the world?"—at first sight looked so hopeless that I did not credit it with a significant following. The more I read, however, and the more I talked with theologians, the more obvious it became that "Honest to

God" and the similarly oriented books—"Soundings," "Objections to Christian Belief," and Werner Pelz's "God Is No More"—were mirrors of the contemporary theological world at large, reflecting, interestingly, even the Archbishop of Canterbury. For although the Archbishop had unequivocally censured not only Robinson and his ideas but his decision to air them in a newspaper prior to book publication, less than two years after the appearance of "Honest to God" Ramsey was himself in print in a rival paper, the *Sunday Times,* with some of Robinson's ideas, which he seemed in the meantime to have casually made his own. Thus, it was soon impressed upon me that the prophets of change were swaying even the high and the mighty, and I was left wondering what would remain of Christianity when the prophecies were fulfilled.

Soon after my conversations in this country with Niebuhr, Tillich, and van Buren, I went to Britain, and continued my quest for knowledge of the New Theology and its proponents in Cambridge and Southwark. It was generally thought that Cambridge and Southwark together formed an axis of new, or "heretical," theology, even though one could hardly imagine two places more dissimilar. Cambridge still managed to keep a little of the character of a market town, set deep in the country, where certain aspects of the twentieth century, like its industry, had hardly been noticed, while Southwark was an impoverished industrial and working-class section of Greater London. Yet Cambridge was the university of nearly all the so-called "Southwark fellow-travellers" and of some non-fellow-travelling Southwark clerics as well, including the diocesan bishop himself; Cambridge was where "Soundings" had originated, the product of a close group of theologians who had been meeting regularly at the university for some years to discuss ideas, and the results of whose discussions were reputed to be as radical in character as any theories knocking about in the theological world.

A Cambridge don I knew said to me, "I think as a rule it's

deplorable when people classify and lump things together, but in the case of Cambridge and Southwark this has some validity. Such radicals as there are, in fact, can be met with in these two places, and all of them got their education at Cambridge during the flowering here of a sort of second humanism—remember Robinson's emphasis on rationalism and love—and all of them found the world outside, when they had to go out into it, something of a shock. Perhaps partly because of this, and partly because Oxford philosophy has never had much influence at Cambridge, another characteristic of the radicals is philosophical confusion. You see, the faculties here are so isolated from one another that the Tripos of Moral Sciences has got narrower and narrower. Antony Flew, now at the University of Keele, once read a paper to a Moral Science society here in which he uttered the name 'Plato,' and it was as though he had uttered a four-letter word. Ancients and Moderns aren't mixed here, as they are at Oxford. At Cambridge, Plato is studied only in the Classics faculty. There has always been a touch of King's College religion about Cambridge—the very beautiful King's Chapel, with its very beautiful choir, where anyone, religious or not, would like to go to church—which means a touch of intellectualism and eccentricity. For instance, Richard Braithwaite, who is a professor of Moral Philosophy here, was persuaded—philosophically—to become a Christian in his adult life, but, apparently, only after an exchange of several letters between him and the church. He certainly behaved as though a private treaty had been made, with a table of exemptions for him, and everyone in Cambridge believed that this was so. When he was baptized, practically everybody who was anybody in Cambridge was there, except Wittgenstein."

Yet my friend, upon being pushed, was unable to name any radicals. In fact, in his opinion almost all the men whose names were bandied about in the newspapers as Cambridge radicals—besides Vidler, Williams, MacKinnon, and Bezzant, there were Howard Eugene Root, Fellow and Dean of Emmanuel, and Reverend Canon Hugh William Montefiore, Vicar of Great St. Mary's, Cambridge (before that, Fellow and Dean of Gonville and Caius)—were conservatives of one stripe or another. My friend said, "Vidler is a church historian, not a theologian, and was for a long time an Anglo-Catholic, and a lot of that still sticks to him. Williams, I suppose, is a radical, but he tries things on his pulses, and he often paints with words, to evoke the maximum response. He was in psychoanalysis for a number of years, and talks about it. This is his honesty. MacKinnon is mostly conservative, and he is such a monologuist that he was never even considered for the 'Soundings' discussion group. Bezzant's appearance in 'Objections to Christian Belief' was surprising. He belongs to the previous generation, and his ideas are set. Montefiore has left academic life. Root hasn't written much. He just had time off to write, but he went as an observer to the Vatican Council instead."

Still, Vidler, as the editor of "Soundings," was referred to everywhere as a "midwife" of theology, and not only of theology at Cambridge but of theology in England at large, because for a quarter of a century he had edited the most important journal of the discipline, called *Theology*. For the last ten years or so, he has been Dean of King's College, and therefore, as a matter of course, the high pundit of that King's College religion. No one interested in theological matters goes up to Cambridge without paying his respects to Vidler, and when I went along for my darshana, I discovered that he lived on Staircase X, near the Backs and at the opposite end of the college from E. M. Forster. On the front door of his rooms, which were a few flights up, there was a sign asking visitors to walk in and knock at the door of an inner room. I followed instructions, and, upon being bidden to enter the inner sanctum, found Vidler, a massive man with a neatly trimmed white beard and enormous black eyebrows, sitting on a sofa. He was wearing a black shirt, a black collar, and a white tie, in the fashion of eminent divines of old, before the era of the dog collar. He was, in fact, a study in black and white, but, surprisingly, a bottle-green corduroy jacket, a purple tie, and a gray fur hat were lying on a chair, making one think that whatever he did had a touch of deliberation about it. On the wall space without books there was a watercolor of Lamb House, where Henry James lived, and over the mantelpiece a collection of about a dozen Staffordshire pottery figures, all of John Wesley. In a corner stood a glass case holding a number of mustache cups, which have not been seen about since the First World War, when soldiers had to shave off their whiskers in order to fight. (The elegance of some of the cups recalled the era of the third Marquis of Salisbury and the eighth Duke of Devonshire, two Victorians remembered for, among other things, their magnificent mustaches, widely emulated.) The windows of Vidler's room looked out on the river and on Clare Bridge, which many consider the loveliest bridge in England.

"It's difficult to discover who the radicals are, exactly," I said when we had exchanged greetings. "For one thing, they don't seem to have written very much."

Vidler had in his hand a large-bowled pipe of the type called a twister. He now crouched down in front of the fireplace, in which a coal fire was burning, and slowly lit the twister with a spill. Having returned to the sofa, he said, "Oh, well, most of them are radicals only in discussion; when people trust each other and meet among friends, they can say things freely. In any case, at Oxford there is the tradition of being learned and putting things out, but at Cambridge the tradition is much more of debating and going over the same thing again and again. Brooke Foss Westcott and F. J. Hort were great nineteenth-century Cambridge theologians, and Hort started many books, but he didn't publish. Well, he did publish a few books, but they weren't the books he really wanted to write. We agonize over everything here, and somehow never get into print. By the way, I decided some time ago not to offer cigarettes, but if you smoke, please go ahead."

I said I didn't smoke.

He got up and fetched from a cupboard a couple of glasses, a bottle of sherry, and some biscuits. Pouring out sherry, he said, "I need only one good meal to survive. Even here at King's, I dine in the Hall only once a day. For the rest of the time, I just take snacks. I don't want to get grossly fat, or anything like that."

Over the sherry, I asked him how the "Soundings" group had got started.

He relit his twister at the fire and said, "Oh, well, when I came back to Cambridge in 1956—I had been an undergraduate here before going on to Wells Theological College and the provinces—I thought there should be some new kind of examination of theological problems. There were philosophical analyses and scientific developments, and I thought we should find out how theology could come to terms with them. Two or three of the younger theologians came and suggested to me that we should form a group for discussion, and we surveyed the available people. We considered Robinson, among others, but excluded him, because we didn't feel that he had the sort of radical attitude we wanted in our group. This was quite a reasonable view at the time, since he was then Dean of Clare and a very conventional New Testament scholar. We didn't include Mac-Kinnon, either."

"Why was that?" I asked.

"Oh, MacKinnon is very good when you get him on his own, but he gets things on his mind. At the moment, it's the Agony of Christ in the Garden of Gethsemane. And everything, whatever MacKinnon is talking about, tends to turn into this Agony. Actually, I got the idea of the 'Soundings' group from the Moot. The Moot was thought up by the theologian J. H. Oldham, who's now ninety. It was the best group I have been a member of, and the most high-powered. In the Moot there were T. S. Eliot, Karl Mannheim, Middleton Murry—people like that. The Moot used to meet for long weekends three or four times a year. We used to sit about in a large room. Oldham would sit on a little stool. He was deaf—of course, he wore a machine—and when someone began talking he would move his little stool next to him. The papers read there were circulated among the members. A very few of them found their way into print. I have a complete set of them. When I retire, I hope to do something with them."

Vidler, who was speaking in a rather offhand monotone, continued, "I'm going to retire in 1967; it's the thing I most look forward to. Then I'll be able to spend a little bit more time on my bees, among other things. I used to collect wild bees; now I collect bees with honey. They're much easier to look after—you don't have to do anything about them for months. I'll retire to Rye, Sussex, where I was brought up. My sister—she's a widow—has bought a house there, and many of my old relatives are settling in Rye again. I'll retire to the family house. It was left to me by my father—he was a great local historian of Rye. It's a part of a thirteenth-century house that has survived. My family has been living in it since 1801. It was rather small for my family when I was young, but it'll be just right for a bachelor like me now. About a hundred and fifty yards from us is Henry James's house. When I was two, he kissed me—that sort of thing. I've frequently lived in beautiful places, like Windsor—I was Canon of St. George's Chapel in Windsor. I also served in the slums of Newcastle upon Tyne and Birmingham for a time."

I looked up Williams next. He lived on the ground floor of a staircase in Trinity Great Court, the largest quadrangle at Cambridge, which, interestingly, had no right angles. He turned out to be a saturnine sort of person with a beet-red face. He was standing thoughtfully in front of a very hot Esse stove in his sitting room. I remarked that it was quite warm there, and he said, "This stove has a history. A couple of years ago, the thermostat went bad, and it burned up fourteen hours of fuel in two hours. This mantelpiece—or, rather, its predecessor—caught fire. I was sleeping in the bedroom over there. Well, I had the door closed, so I didn't smell anything. But then I heard sort of a row going on outside my door, and I came out to look, and the floorboards and the mantelpiece—or, rather, its predecessor—were on fire. I ran to the porter's lodge in my pajamas, and, of course, the fire guard was here in minutes. The College got me a new Esse stove; otherwise, they knew, I might do more damage to their property! This Esse stove has two thermostats. The nice thing about an Esse stove is that it stays hot twenty-four hours."

Lighting a Player's Gold Leaf Virginia cigarette, Williams went on, "Smoking is a sublimated desire for breast-sucking; that's why they haven't been able to wean people off it, in spite of the medical warnings. I was reading in the *Times* this morning that all the fuss about cigarettes has made Americans smoke more. There is also, I suppose, a strong death wish in people. I've tried talking psychology with many dons, and this is quite easy, because quite a few of the dons here are in psychoanalysis, I have discovered. And they have the kind of perception that only psychoanalysis can give one. *I* was in psychoanalysis for a few years. What I learned from psychoanalysis was that what one thought on the conscious level, and thought was sincere, had unconscious origins. Take the Commandment 'Thou shalt love thy neighbor as thyself.' Now, it seems almost too easy, but *I* think you love your neighbor more when you come to know the meaning of Auden's lines 'O stand, stand at the window / As the tears scald and start; / You shall love your crooked neighbor / With your crooked heart.' And Christ says in the parable of the sheep and the goats, in St. Matthew, beginning at 25:32, that people who are not Christians can love just as well, and perhaps love more deeply. But the New Testament is full of appeals to the guilt in man. This I want to get away from."

He continued in this vein for some time.

I could not bring myself to say farewell to Cambridge without exchanging greetings with Donald MacKinnon, not because he had been passed over for "Soundings" and was a monologuist— I was partial to him on both counts—but because I had made his acquaintance some years before, in connection with something I was writing at the time, and found him to be a good, almost riveting talker. Now MacKinnon was giving lectures on the philosophy of religion, in which he grappled with the Continental theologians—Barth, Bultmann, and Bonhoeffer—and tried to formulate certain propositions, or "truth conditions," to serve as a sort of litmus-paper test for believers. I invited MacKinnon to dine with me at my hotel, and he arrived wearing a duplicate of the bottle-green corduroy jacket in Vidler's room. He ordered jellied madrilène, steak-and-kidney pie, and a large glass of ginger beer with lemon. Then he slowly brought out of a pocket a pencil and a double-edged blade, but he didn't set to work and sharpen the pencil. I remembered from our previous meeting that while he was soliloquizing he had absently whittled a pencil to a long, thin point and then held the pencil by the point between two fingers. The pencil had appeared very fragile, the exposed lead appearing to be always on the verge of breaking. Eventually, however, the pencil had simply slipped out of his hand, and he had reached for another and proceeded to go through the motions all over again.

Now the pencil and blade remained frozen in his hands as I questioned him about his truth conditions.

He began slowly, enunciating every word as though he were lecturing to a class of dedicated note-takers. "The truth conditions are certain kinds of propositions which a Christian has to

believe in order to be a Christian. For example, I would say"—
there was a long pause—"God exists. Sorry. Correction. A
Christian must believe there is a movement from God to man
in the historical figure of Jesus of Nazareth, and it is in relation
to Him that faith is asked of men. All right? In His life, death,
and resurrection a decisive act—sorry, a decisive deed—was done.
This deed, which Karl Barth somewhere refers to as 'the great
disturbance,' is significant in time and in eternity. In the Church,
which is a part of human history, men and women are effectively
reminded of this Person: what He is, what He has done, and
what He does. The organ of this recollection is called the Holy
Spirit. But it is also given determinate shape and content by
the Sacrament. This example of the movement from God to
man in the figure of Jesus that I have given you off the cuff
requires, as you see, a great deal of qualification and development. Some of the expressions in it are quite liberally vague.
To make myself absolutely clear, by a truth condition of a
proposition I mean another proposition, which must be true if
the proposition in question is to be called true. For instance,
there are six books on the corner of this table. If that is true,
it is true if, and only if, there are six books on the corner of
this table—if there are five books it is false, if there is a sack
of potatoes it is false, if there are twenty-five books it is false.
Do you see what I mean? Now, as I have demonstrated, Christianity is false if Jesus of Nazareth did not exist. Right? Therefore, the proposition 'Jesus of Nazareth existed' is among the
truth conditions of Christianity. There are other truth conditions—and two follow which are definitely controversial. One,
that in the explanation of His death Jesus in some sense knew—
that is, could formulate in words to Himself, which could be
intelligible in theory to others—what He sought to accomplish.
All right? According to the Synoptics—that is, the first three
Gospels—He performed certain actions, which admittedly are
variously described, over bread and wine in the upper room at

the last meal He took with His disciples, which may or may not have been a Passover. Now, by these actions He seemed to imply that He did in some sense know what He was about. If we must say that in no sense whatever did He know what He was about, then it seems to me that Christianity is false. The second controversial truth condition—it seems to me that Christianity stands or falls by the finding empty of the tomb during the thirty-six hours or so after the death of Jesus on the Cross. Now, the time is unimportant. If the empty tomb was shown to be false, then I would have to abandon what I call my faith. Now, I want to be very careful here. Indeed, I do not—repeat, *not*—identify the empty tomb with the Resurrection. I do not. It is a sign of the Resurrection. I would go further and say that its being emptied of its occupant— No, another way: The event is an element in the Resurrection, but the Resurrection itself, the Father raising the Son from the dead, although in my view it entails the emptying of the tomb, is not identical with that emptying. In other words, there is a very simple piece of logic here: The proposition 'This is a red square' entails the proposition 'This is red,' but the proposition 'This is a red square' is not identical with proposition 'This is red.' All right? The empty tomb, then, is a sign that the Resurrection was accomplished in time and space, in a truly human environment. It is therefore a sign that is seen for what it is—that death must be itself annihilated. I don't feel the same way about—attach the same importance to—the Second Coming, because that's too incredible, nor would I include the Virgin Birth in my list of truth conditions. Where the Virgin Birth is concerned, all I would say is that I think this matter is frequently discussed today with an absence of true theological seriousness. There are very important questions in regard to the Virgin Birth which have to be thrashed out, but I prefer to call myself agnostic on that point."

MacKinnon shifted the pencil in his hand, but he didn't begin sharpening it. He continued, "You see, there is a query here about the Virgin Birth—whether such a birth withdraws Christ from the conditions of ordinary human existence. There are, you see, critical and exegetical problems here. To go on, where these truth conditions are concerned, someone like Bultmann is half Christian and half not. Sometimes he emphatically is not. In fact, I doubt if he ever is, insofar as the empty tomb is concerned. He does nearly meet some of my other truth conditions, however. I know I have been sounding like a conservative politician being asked if he or a colleague of his is center, left of center, or right of center on an important issue."

Indeed, I thought, the truth conditions had turned out to be as arbitrary as anything else (if the Second Coming was incredible for MacKinnon, why shouldn't the empty tomb be incredible for Bultmann?), but MacKinnon was off on his favorite topic at that time, the Agony of Christ in the Garden of Gethsemane. "We must substitute for abstract general statements concerning the being and purposes of God and of men statements that show them in terms of, or set them in relation to, Jesus Christ," he said. "We cannot speak of something called the Christian doctrine of man without mention of the prayers of Jesus in the wilderness, on the hillside, and in the garden. Of his compassion for the leper and for the blind, for the tax gatherer and for the prostitute. Of his inexorable sternness toward scribe and Pharisee, the self-righteous heart turned in upon itself. We certainly cannot write of that doctrine of man without, as it were, setting at the heart of our page the laconic, cynical double-entendre of Pilate, '*Ecce homo!*'—'Behold the man!' The impossibility here is a logical possibility. Its disregard is sheer self-contradiction. Is that clear?"

For the first time, it was beginning not to be, possibly because MacKinnon, being very familiar with the theme, had started using a shorthand of his own. There was no retrieving the conversation from the Garden of Gethsemane, though our dinner went on for some time.

Most commentators have credited both the soul-searching and the conclusions of "Honest to God" to Robinson's experiences in Southwark, a central borough of London on the South Bank of the Thames and connected with the City of London by Blackfriars, London, and Southwark bridges. The borough has a population of about a hundred thousand and an area of a little less than two square miles. (Actually, the diocese of Southwark covers the whole of South London and half of Surrey, which together now have a population of about two and a half million.) Southwark takes its name from the southward works, or fortifications, of London (numerous Roman remains have been found in the area), and though very few historical monuments survive, it is rich in associations—particularly the district bordering the Thames. Here once stood the Bear and the Paris Gardens (used for the popular sports of bearbaiting and bullbaiting), the Globe Theatre, and numerous inns, among which was the Tabard, mentioned by Chaucer in "The Canterbury Tales," and numerous prisons, including Marshalsea, in which Dickens' father was confined. Southwark is also famous for its beautiful diocesan cathedral, of thirteenth- and fourteenth-century origin, which was restored in the nineteenth century and is now called the Cathedral and Collegiate Church of St. Saviour and St. Mary Overie (it contains the graves of the poet Lawrence Fletcher and of Shakespeare's brother Edmund), and for such old established institutions as Guy's Hospital and Bethlehem, Royal Hospital for the Insane (whence the corruption "bedlam"). In spite of some recent success on the part of real-estate agents in making part of that district on the bank of the river more chic by advertising it as South Chelsea, Southwark as a whole gives the impression of one dirty, mean street after another, and one critic of "Honest to God," perhaps taking his cue more from the evidence of poverty than from the facts of radicalism in the clergy, wrote, "London south of the Thames has become the Red Belt of the Church of England. Mervyn Stockwood, Bishop of Southwark, is mild enough himself, but he enjoys the company of turbulent priests, and behind every other dog collar in the pulpits under his charge you will as like as not find a secret Aldermaston marcher, a furtive abortion-law reformer, or a militant campaigner for the Socialist Kingdom of God. That is the environment in which Dr. John Robinson, Suffragan Bishop of Woolwich (a division of Southwark), wrote 'Honest to God.'" As far as I could find out, "every other dog collar in the pulpits" referred to, at most, a couple of dozen clerics (altogether there were five hundred and forty clergymen holding full-time appointments in Southwark), who, it was true, had made enough noise in the press to sound like a few hundred, especially to the ear of a writer for the English weekly the *Tribune,* which pictures itself as "political, literary, with Socialist outlook." In any case, the weekly is not known for its devotional writings. These ecclesiasts had made their presence felt by taking stands on several questions of varying religious importance: Canon John D. Pearce-Higgins, Vice-Provost of Southwark Cathedral, by refusing to sign the Thirty-nine Articles; Canon Douglas Rhymes by, as one of his colleagues put it, "trying to reconcile the Church's morality with modern psychology. The trouble there is that if he says sexual intercourse outside marriage is not necessarily sinful, the ill-informed take this to mean, 'O.K., chaps, we can all do it;'" the Reverend Dr. Eric James, the director of Parish and People, an association of churchmen concerned with modern solutions to pastoral problems, by going around the country to raise "the banner of radical reform;" and the Rector of St. Mary's, Woolwich, Nicolas Stacey, and a cluster of satellites by trying to make a more worldly place of his Church of St. Mary, which serves a parish of twelve thousand people, most of them living in houses built by the London County Council.

I had first made Robinson's acquaintance through the newspapers in 1960, in connection with the case known as Regina v. Penguin Books, Ltd., in which the firm was arraigned for its publication of "Lady Chatterley's Lover." In that celebrated trial, which will surely be remembered as one of the most bizarre episodes in literary history, the Bishop had done a brilliant turn or two for the defense. After Mr. Gerald Gardiner, Q.C., the counsel for the defense (four years later he became Lord Chancellor in the present Labour government), had asked the Bishop a series of questions designed to impress on the jury the witness's accomplishments—that he had been up at Cambridge; that he had read Classics there, and taken a First in theology and a Doctorate of Philosophy; and that his ordination had necessarily involved him in a special study of ethics—the Bishop was faced with the question "Is this a book which in your view Christians ought to read?"

"Yes, I think it is," the Bishop had answered.

"What do you say are the ethical merits of the book?" Mr. Gardiner had asked.

"I would not want to be put in a position of arguing this primarily on its ethical merits," Robinson had said. "Clearly, Lawrence did not have a Christian valuation of sex, and the kind of sexual relationship depicted in the book is not one that I would necessarily regard as ideal, but what I think is clear is that what Lawrence is trying to do is to portray the sex relationship as something essentially sacred. Archbishop William Temple . . . once said that Christians do not make jokes about sex for the same reason that they do not make jokes about Holy Communion, not because it is sordid but because it is sacred, and I think Lawrence tried to portray this relation as in a real sense something sacred, as in a real sense an act of holy communion."

The debate might be narrowly about "Lady Chatterley," but it was also about Christian morals in general, or so it appeared from a sort of sideshow that was soon put on view in the Christian world. The *Church Times* editorialized:

Sex in Christian marriage is a communion, and it is holy. Adultery is not. Lawrence passionately believed in the most powerful tenet of most pagan religions, that sex in itself is the ultimate divinity. It was precisely against that corrupting belief that the Christian Church fought and won its long battle in the Roman Empire. . . . That is why it calls for the strongest possible protest, all the more since a bishop is thought to speak for the Church: the man cannot divorce himself from the office.

The Bishop had landed in the dock with Lady Chatterley. He replied in a public letter: "For the record, I should like to stress that I did not capitalise these last two words ["holy communion"]. . . . I did not say that *I* thought the relationship between Lady Chatterley and Mellors was an act of holy communion. For the Christian no adulterous union could be so described. . . . To some, of course, the mere juxtaposition of sex and the Holy Communion has seemed blasphemous. I can only reply that the Bible, both in the Old and New Testament, is full of language which uses the most intimate relation between man and woman as the image of God's union with his people."

If Robinson had hedged a little on the particular issue of "Lady Chatterley" and "holy communion," he was subsequently shown to me to be a supporter of many liberal causes. He was a campaigner against capital punishment, on the ground that in Christianity no man was irredeemable; a liturgical innovator (at Clare College, Cambridge, of which he was Dean from 1951 to 1959, the Communion was followed by a communal breakfast at which, under his direction, the unconsecrated portion of the Offertory bread—a loaf baked in the college—was consumed with butter and marmalade); an advocate of granting burial rites to suicides, on the ground that suicide was a social sin and a failure of the whole society; a reformer of clerical stipends; and a member of the Homosexual Law Reform Society.

Now and then, to further these causes and interpret the real meaning of Christianity today, he took to journalism, as when he wrote for the *Sunday Mirror* an article that appeared under the title "Did the Miracles Really Happen?" "A miracle-monger, a magic-man, a god in human clothes who could have done anything He liked, if He'd really wanted to?" Robinson wrote. "The impression made by Jesus's teaching was precisely that He was, as we should say, as good as His word. 'What is this? A new kind of teaching! He speaks with authority. When He gives orders, even the unclean spirits submit.' This was love, not merely in talk, but in action, changing the stunted, tortured lives of men, women and children. . . . Or take the feeding of the multitude, when apparently 5,000 were fed as a result of one boy coming out with his sandwiches. . . . That's what love can do."

A sequel to "Did the Miracles Really Happen?," in the next issue of the *Sunday Mirror,* was entitled "It's That Man Again!" and it contended, in the Bishop's unmistakable cadences:

People think the Church teaches that one afternoon—this year, next year, sometime—Telstar will pick up a picture of Christ descending from the skies with thousands of angels in train, returning to earth to judge the world. . . .

The Second Coming is not something that can be caught by radar or seen on a screen. . . .

To get this truth across, the Bible draws pictures—to make it easier on the imagination.

Thus, there is the familiar picture (painted in glorious Technicolor) of the whole world suddenly being flooded with the presence of Christ—as we should say, "out of the blue." . . .

At any moment, when you least expect it, He may come into your life, like a burglar at dead of night, or the boss walking in when you thought he was on the other side of the world.

This is Jesus speaking, as he constantly did, in parables. No one supposes He'll *literally* knock on the door this evening or enter the office tomorrow morning.

But it makes us stop and think. Suppose our everyday lives were suddenly crossed by His, what should we make of Him or He of us? . . .

To skin your eyes watching the skies for the return of Christ is as misguided as to wait for the archaeologists to dig up evidence for the fall of Adam. For both are ways of trying to make vivid what Christians believe is true, not just of one moment but of every moment. [The italics are the *Sunday Mirror's*.] . . .

Always, at every turn, *"It's that Man again!"* (I chose that title for the first TV programme I ever did, but it was banned by the ITA as blasphemous!)

"Honest to God" was, in a sense, a blending of all these ingredients, including the remains of scholarly interests that had made his early reputation in the narrow but solid world of scholarship, which had been achieved, in some measure, by his avoiding theory, punditry, and public controversy and devoting himself, with brilliant results, to a textual study of the New Testament—a work, in its way, no different from that of any scholar, whatever his field. To find out exactly how "Honest to God" had been prepared, I now went to the Student Christian Movement Press, of London, which is one of the more influential publishing houses in the world of theology, to meet the Reverend David L. Edwards, its managing director and chief editor, and Robinson's publisher. The offices of the SCM Press, situated in Bloomsbury Street, seemed to reflect the halfway status between scholarship and commerce that publishing enjoys, and so, in some degree, did Edwards, a rather donnish figure who nevertheless had a slight air of the publicity man about him.

Edwards scarcely needed a question about "Honest to God" to set him off.

"Our first edition of 'Honest to God' was only six thousand copies," he told me, sitting in front of a gas fire in his office. "I had not found the book all that new. We had been publishing books saying similar things for some time; we had published Bultmann and Tillich and Bonhoeffer. But John Robinson was not a Herr Professor. Tillich and Bultmann were both Herr Professor—Herr Professor is something very big and formal—and Tillich and Bultmann would not stoop to saying things in a personal way, as John Robinson said he had difficulty with prayer. Bultmann's books about demythologizing Christianity contained words like '*kerygma*' and 'myth.' But '*kerygma*' is a Greek word for 'preaching,' and not very many ordinary men know about the word, and he was using the word 'myth' also in a special way—not as an ordinary man uses 'myth,' to say something is untrue. I had known Ivan Yates, a correspondent for the *Observer,* when we were at Oxford, and had kept up with him after going down. I sent him the proofs of 'Honest to God,' with the idea that he might be able to make a little article out of it for the *Observer,* but he sent back the proofs, saying that the book was too theological for the *Observer.* The book was to be published on a Tuesday, and the Saturday but one before that Tuesday Ivan Yates rang me up and said that their main feature for the Sunday before the publication of the book had fallen through, and could John Robinson fill the gap? The Monday after Ivan Yates rang me, he went to see John Robinson, and John Robinson wrote his article, and submitted it two days later. It was printed just as he submitted it, without any changes. I didn't see the article until I opened my *Observer,* and when I saw the headline 'Our Image of God Must Go,' I knew there would be a storm—and the book would sell. John Robinson already had the reputation among journalists of being a bishop who made good copy. He'd got that during the Chatterley trial. Also, other people had been asking questions such as 'Why do unbreakable Christian rules always turn out to be about sex and not about war?'—or the one made on the B.B.C., 'In Christianity, is chastity the highest virtue?'—and such questions had been making the rounds for some time. Others had been asking the question: Was love more important than law? And: Was charity more important than punishment? And John Robinson was, of course, dealing with some of these questions. Later, there was also quite a lot of talk about sex in connection with Christine Keeler—another reason for the continuing success of 'Honest to God.' In a way, sex and the transcendence of God are connected—they are both difficult to speak about. But you must talk to John Robinson. I am much more conservative than John Robinson, and he is always saying that I'm trying to make him out to be more conservative than he is."

Before seeing Robinson, however, I decided to seek out his chief pastor, the Archbishop of Canterbury, and ascertain his views. When I called Lambeth Palace, which has been the main residence of the Archbishop from ancient times, in order to request an audience, I was handed over to his public-relations officer, a gentleman who identified himself as Colonel R. J. A. Hornby, O.B.E., M.I.P.R. (Member of the Institute of Public Relations). After I had explained my purpose, the Colonel said heartily, "We have very good relations with the press, and I am sure the Archbishop would like to see you. But the Archbishop has not got much small talk. You say to him, 'Your Grace, I am here to get your views on X,' and then he will talk on it. He doesn't go in for 'How are you?' and 'How do you like the weather?' He is known to sit through dinners without saying a word to a dinner partner, on his right, left, or across. I remember the time a publisher of a New York newspaper came over from America to see the Archbishop. They simply sat and stared at each other for fifteen minutes. Luckily, I had the London correspondent of the same newspaper with me, so we chatted and they listened. I warn you, even after you ask him a serious question, there can be long silences. This can go on for quite some time. Sometimes he overdoes the brevity. In the Lords, for example, I think that his speeches are really too short—though, mind you, in the Lords you've got to be short! And most of the things he writes now are like that—short. Also, because he is both a spiritual and a political leader, the context in which he makes his remarks is very important. You might put the question to the Archbishop 'Does Your Grace believe in the Virgin Birth?' and he might say 'No,' but unless you knew the theological arguments behind his answer you might get the Archbishop wrong. You might ask the Archbishop 'Do agnostics go to Heaven?' and he might say 'Yes'—as indeed he would say 'Yes'—but, again, unless you knew the theological arguments you might get him wrong."

I assured Colonel Hornby that I knew something of the theological arguments he had cited, and within a day or two he called to confirm my appointment at Lambeth Palace. The Colonel gave me a sort of dossier on his chief. I learned that Ramsey was born in 1904; was nurtured at Repton, where his immediate predecessor in the see of Canterbury, Geoffrey Fisher, was then headmaster; went up to Cambridge, where he was President of the Union; studied theology at Cuddesdon; and went on to an unfaltering career in the ecclesiastical hierarchy, as, successively, curate, examining chaplain, Vicar of St. Benedict's Church, Cambridge, Canon of Durham Cathedral, Professor of Divinity at Durham University, Regius Professor of Divinity at Cambridge, Bishop of Durham, and Archbishop of York, acceding to the see of Canterbury in 1961. He was married, he had no children, and he was the author of such highly esteemed works as "The Gospel and the Catholic Church," "The Resurrection of Christ," and "The Glory of God and the Transfiguration of Christ."

Lambeth Palace lies south of the Thames, near Westminster Bridge, diagonally across from the Houses of Parliament, and not far from such monuments to the modern age as the Imperial Chemical Industries Building and the Vickers Building. The palace itself, furthermore, is a patchwork of periods old and new. The study in which the Archbishop received me gave a similar impression, for the books were old, the bookcases new. Otherwise, there was nothing particularly memorable about it. It had a bay window overlooking the vast enclosed gardens of the Palace, a large, dusty desk in one corner, and little piles of paper on tables here and there, as though the Archbishop did his work wherever he happened to be sitting. The Archbishop himself looked like one's idea of Elijah. He was big and had a high-domed, craggy forehead, a certain amount of white hair, and shaggy eyebrows. He was dressed in a cassock, and was seated, with his shoulders hunched, in an upholstered chair by the fire.

"Yes, yes, yes, yes, yes," he said as I entered, and then, unwinding himself, rose to greet me. He offered me his hand from above, in the old-fashioned manner, turning his wrist in such a way that his fingers pointed straight down. "Yes, yes, yes, yes, yes," he said, and reoccupied his seat.

Fearing that the conversation might already have ground to a halt, I said, "Your Grace, I would like to know your views on 'Honest to God.'"

"Yes, yes, yes, yes, yes, 'Honest to God.'" The Archbishop fell silent. "I *think* that it has *been* some help in the quarters where not many *people* believed in *God*," he said, finally. He had a way of emphasizing the most unexpected word.

"And those quarters where God was already believed in, Your Grace?"

"Yes, yes, yes, yes, yes, there, too," he said.

I asked how, in his opinion, the dialogue between Christianity and the secular world could best be carried on.

"I think God is to be found within the secular world, and this is an important fact to realize," he said. "But the main function of the Church is to bring Christians together in a community."

"Can the apparatus of the Church ever be a hindrance, Your Grace, to the community of Christians?"

"It could be. It is said that there are churches every four hundred yards in England, but in places that are overpopulated there are not enough churches, and there are certainly not enough churches in the world."

I turned back to the theme of "Honest to God," and his initial hostile reaction to it, his subsequent appraisal of it (some had attributed the confusion to his wish to safeguard such delicate progress as has recently been made toward an Anglican and Catholic rapprochement), and, finally, his seeming adoption of some of Robinson's language.

"I speak differently to different kinds of audiences," he replied. "To people in the university, who are intelligent, I speak in one way; to other people I speak in another way. Everyone has tricks of speech, and they're different for different people. I am not self-conscious enough to know what my tricks of speech are. I have read the people Robinson relies on. Yes, yes, yes, yes, yes. I have read Bultmann. I think I could take an examination on Bultmann. I think his demythologization is based on the fact that he thinks the primitive Christians did not take history as seriously as I think they took history. I think we ought to take history very seriously, because the primitive Christians took history very seriously. I've got a very good grip on Bonhoeffer. In a pamphlet I wrote on Bonhoeffer, I maintain a balance between religionless Christianity—between what Bonhoeffer says—and what the Church is. I could not pass an examination on Tillich, but I have read and reread Barth many times and I have a good grip on his commentary on the Romans, but his 'Dogmatics' I cannot read—that's very English of me. I value Barth as a prophet but not as a dogmatist. When John Robinson gets cornered, he uses the old traditional imagery—like the hands of God—but the thing is that I use traditional imagery when I'm not cornered; that is the difference. Some of the best criticism of his book was written by Roman Catholics. The reason that Roman Catholic criticisms of him were good was that some of the things he was saying had already been said by the Christian mystics. There is a mystical tradition in Christianity. When there is blackness about the images of God, there is finally an illumina-tion. I think in some ways John Robinson is talking about this blackness; he wants to get away from thinking about the images of God, to get beyond it, to get beyond this blackness. I think there are generations of Christians who go through this black-ness, but eventually there is another illumination. John Robinson is a good New Testament scholar, but he doesn't know very much about mysticism or philosophy. Yes, yes, yes, yes, yes, Robinson did have a contribution to make. But they talk about South Bank religion; they talk about the Cambridge Movement. Now, I was at Cambridge, and I live here in this house on the South Bank, and I don't have any South Bank religion and I don't belong to any Cambridge Movement. John Robinson him-self is conservative in some ways and very radical in others. Vidler is conservative in some ways and radical in others. The trouble is that everyone puts all these people together. There is no such thing as South Bank religion or the Cambridge Move-ment."

I wondered if the Archbishop's office stood in the way of what he could say, and I asked him whether it was ever a burden to him.

"My office is not a heavy burden," he said. "That would be the moaner's way of thinking about the office. I have my diocese in Canterbury, I have there the duties of a large bishopric, and they take up time. But I'm not a moaner. I don't worry about my duties, and because of that I'm very cheerful."

"Does Your Grace find certain doctrines more difficult to defend than others?" I asked.

"I don't moan about my doctrinal worries, either. Yes, yes, yes, yes, yes, I would have to go through all of the New Testament, and some doctrines I would have to say were rationalizations, and others I would say are not. I believe the empty tomb was not a rationalization. I think the Resurrection was an event. It was to tell us that Christ is still alive as ever."

Robinson lives at 17 Manor Way, Blackheath, a suburb of London. When I went to call on him, I hired a car—he lived an hour's ride from where I was putting up—and a driver, who, by an odd coincidence, turned out to be a native of Blackheath. "So you're going to meet the Bishop," he said. "I am always going up to his house, and if you don't mind my saying so, in my opinion he's not the bishop I would have chosen as my bishop. He's futuristic—radical, or something. Anyway, a bishop should be at least ten years older than he is, and much mellower. Now, I agree the Church has to change. It's not modern enough. There are these large, drafty rooms. It's not like home. But he's too contradictory, or something."

The parishioner talked on in a disconnected way, and after a time we turned onto a dirt road and arrived at a large red brick house with a large garden. This was the Bishop's house. When I rang the bell, a boyish-faced man dressed in a dark-blue suit, a mauve tie, and a white shirt half opened the door and looked out. "I am Woolwich," he said. "I can't get the door open any farther, because my wife is painting the hall. If you turn sideways, you can get in."

I managed to get in through the Bishop's door. He pointed to a figure in a mackintosh high up on a ladder, and said, "This is my wife, Ruth—she is doing some redecorating, and we have also discovered that the whole house has to be rewired for electricity. None of it is earthed at the moment."

"Be careful, John, paint might drip on you!" his wife called from the ladder. "Just move a little to the right. Keep close to the wall."

The Bishop led the way into a nondescript, littered study, shut the door behind him, and sat down in a chair and chuckled, for no apparent reason.

I asked him how he was surviving the debate over "Honest to God," which was continuing, and, indeed, had been given an added impetus by the announcement that a new book of his, "The New Reformation?," would appear shortly.

The Bishop cocked his head toward a row of books along a side wall and said, "These are all either translations of 'Honest to God' or books in which 'Honest to God' is mentioned. Over there, across the room, is a shelfful of scrapbooks of reviews and letters, and this mountain on the floor is some more reviews and letters, which haven't yet been filed away. I did a blitz this morning and got at least half of them cleared up. I occasionally do a blitz, but they keep on coming." His voice was, for the most part, expressionless, his manner mild. "I was able to find time to write 'Honest to God' because of a bad back. To tell you the truth, I was doing nothing more strenuous than bending down to tie my shoelaces, and I got a strained back. I simply stayed in bed for three months and wrote most of the book. When 'Honest to God' was first suggested as a title, I was against it, because it was too flippant, but now I see it was a good title, refreshing and striking; the phrase has since changed its meaning a bit in the English language. Since the book appeared, requests for lectures and interviews have kept coming every day. I have had difficulty finding time to work on my new book. I happened to finish a lecture on atheism—it's called 'Can a Truly Contemporary Person *Not* Be an Atheist?'—at the same time as the book, and I added the lecture to the book as an appendix, along with an article my wife wrote, called 'Spiritual Education in a World Without Religion.' I have already given the lecture on atheism in Germany, Sweden, Norway, and Denmark. Here in England, I gave the lecture as a broadcast on the Third Programme. Both the main Sunday papers, the *Observer* and the *Sunday Times,* want to carry it, but I have decided this time to let the *Sunday Times* have it, as I don't want to be associated in the public mind only with one Sunday newspaper."

Edwards had given me a set of proofs of "The New Reformation?" and I had read the lecture on atheism. Most of it seemed to be a variation on "Honest to God." In addition, it suffered, I felt, from the same deficiencies that "Honest to God" did. Among other things, the case for atheism was argued better than the case for Christianity.

I said his book seemed not only to be written for different audiences but also to have been written by two different authors, and I asked if he had any reply to the charge that "Honest to God" was muddled.

"It's a matter of generations," he said. "I dedicated 'Honest to God' to Stephen and Catherine—my teen-age children—and their generation. The older people think I am muddled. They reacted to 'Honest to God' early on. They were set, and they had their own system and ideas. But I have got a vast number of letters from all sorts of people. Many of them said that they had felt the kind of things I was saying. Some of them had never been able to articulate their feelings, didn't know themselves what they felt, and 'Honest to God,' they said, had articulated their feelings for them."

But his correspondents, however many, might have been muddled themselves, I said.

"Now, everyone agrees that Vidler writes with great distinction," the Bishop said. "He's the editor of *Theology* and he has published many radical authors, but he has never taken a definite position. I think if you want to get anywhere you have to be prepared to take a stand. I am not a philosopher, I have never studied any linguistic philosophy, but I have accepted an invitation to go to a Language of Religion Conference up in Durham to debate with Antony Flew, who *is* a philosopher, and whom I admire."

I said some critics had argued that in "Honest to God" he had lumped together people who had nothing in common, most notably his three main sources—Tillich, Bultmann, and Bonhoeffer.

"When I think about it—and I haven't reread the book since I read it in proofs—perhaps the most original thing about the book was combining Bonhoeffer, Tillich, and Bultmann," he said. "In fact, they *are* very different. Tillich says everything is religious, Bonhoeffer wants to do away with religion. Tillich comes from the Hegelian, idealistic tradition, and Bonhoeffer—well, he has nothing in common with this tradition. But they speak to the modern man."

I turned next to a point some critics had made about Robinson's being a radical with the radicals and an orthodox with the orthodox, and chose at random a question on which Robinson had hedged—the physical resurrection of Christ—to ask him about.

"I think the question of whether the tomb was empty is a secondary problem. The heart of the resurrection belief was the conviction that Christ was no longer a dead historical memory but a living presence. Compared with that, the question of exactly what happened to the body, or of how physical or psychological were the appearances, is of minor significance. I would say the same is true also of the Virgin Birth and the Ascension, where the center of interest is not the physical details of what did or did not happen but the conviction which they express about the significance of this man Jesus as one whose whole life 'came from God and went to God,' as St. John put it. Or take the Christmas story—the skies open up, the angels come, and the star lights the Wise Men to the stable and then halts above it. This is contrary to all we know about stars—but that is not the point. This is picture language attempting to indicate the unique significance for the Gospel writers of this birth at Bethlehem."

"But isn't the point that God can do anything—that He did go against the laws of nature?"

"Well, this is still a secondary problem. The important thing is the experience itself, for the people who felt it. The Gospel writers expressed their experience in these pictorial representations. There was a fairly well-established apocalyptic tradition from the old prophets, for instance, and the Gospel writers saw angels in their dreams. Many of their dreams, visions, and pictures came down from their tradition. But what is important is their feeling about the significance of their experiences."

"But the miracles are described in a very exact way, and at great length, and I should have thought that the experiences told through them would lose something of their importance if the miracles didn't in fact happen," I said.

"We now know that a lot of physical illnesses are caused by psychological problems," Robinson said. "We don't know enough about how Christ performed His miracles. But in my wife's appendix to 'The New Reformation?' she quotes one of our three daughters on how Christ healed Peter's mother-in-law. The mother-in-law was so fed up with Peter's spending all his time going around with Jesus that she got a temperature and took to her bed. But when Peter brought Christ to the house and she saw what sort of person her son-in-law had been following, then she wanted to—she did—get up and start doing things for people. I think my daughter got fairly close to the heart of that miracle. But that doesn't mean that I don't believe in the miracles."

I saw my opportunity to bring up the criticism most often

made of the Bishop—that he wanted both to refuse his cake and to have it—and asked if he would care to take a stand on whether the miracles did or did not actually happen.

"That's a secondary problem," he said.

"Then what would you say is a primary one?" I asked.

"The primary concern should be the power of love that Christ exhibited," he said. "Christ showed, as no one has shown before or since, the power of love. Matthew, Mark, and Luke are very important to us as accounts of witnesses to this unique revelation, and the importance of the Bible for us derives from its apostolic tradition. There is, of course, a core of history in Christianity, and that Christ was born in Bethlehem is a historical statement. But there's a difference between historical and theological statements. That Christ was the Son of God is a theological statement, and the way the Gospel writers used it was their expression—their representation—of the life of Jesus."

The telephone rang. Robinson answered it, and after he hung up he remarked, "That on the telephone was a clergyman of mine who has been charged with homosexuality. This is the kind of surroundings in which I must do my theology. The Church has been very good with words about homosexuality, but hasn't done much practically about it. I am on a committee to reform the law, but it would mean more if the Church gave a thousand pounds a year, say, to try to get a reformed law on the books."

Over tea and biscuits, served hurriedly by his wife, Robinson talked, rather shyly, about his distinguished clerical and academic connections, which had made his career as a don and a cleric almost inevitable. Both his father and his maternal grandfather had been canons of Canterbury Cathedral. The relatives of his maternal grandfather, who had also been principal of St. Edmund's Hall, had gone to Oxford, so his brother had gone to Oxford, while he, John, had gone to Cambridge, because his father's relatives had their roots in that university. He had one sister, and she was at present teaching physical training at Roedean, the well-known girls' school. His brother was in Zambia, where he was headmaster of a government school. He had thought that he would never live down the "Chatterley" episode, but, with "Honest to God," he had—so completely that in the records of his chroniclers "Chatterley" didn't even rank as Row No. 1 anymore. Just the other day, his wife had shown him a cutting from the Manchester *Evening News & Chronicle*—a story about his new book—headlined " 'HONEST TO GOD' BISHOP ON WAY TO ROW NO. 2?"

Subsequent mornings brought a *Sunday Times* with Robinson's picture splashed over the front page of the magazine section, and many more newspapers with reviews of "The New Reformation?" (like one in the *Observer:* "A bolshie bishop is so rare that he cannot go unnoticed, and Dr. Robinson is a twentieth-century Lollard airing truths without which the Church must soon suffocate"). Then came satirical pieces, among them

> "Lord I believe, help Thou
> Mine unbelief" is now,
> Prayingwise, dead and gone.
> Now, says the honest Bish.,
> The Christian can but pray:
> "Lord, I'll believe one day
> (I think (I hope (I wish)))."

And, finally, there was the most cherished literary form of all, however debatable its intellectual merits—the omnipresent letter to the editor ("In order to encourage people to swim and to be self-reliant, he is pushing thousands off the raft of faith into the stormy seas of doubt. The pastoral question is whether the casualties will exceed the conquests. Theologically the vital question is whether belief in a transcendental God is a normal preliminary to faith in Christ. All but the most discerning readers might think that the American wisecrack: 'There is no God and Jesus is His Son,' summed up his point of view").

I had first come across the rector Nicolas Stacey, perhaps the most vocal member of the group that deafened the *Tribune* writer, when it was proclaimed that he had added a new dimension to Robinson's revolutionary ideas by putting them into practice—a proclamation made in the more intellectual press, whose church editors seemed to go out of their way to play up church mavericks, perhaps because it confirmed the essentially agnostic point of view of their papers, or perhaps simply because it made a good story. A correspondent for the *Guardian* wrote at some length about how Stacey and his group had become the spearhead of a movement to raise church attendance in Southwark, because Mervyn Stockwood, when he took over the diocese, had faced a situation in which only one-half of one per cent of the population attended his riverside churches, while the national average was ten per cent. The correspondent's approval of Stacey's work seemed to be based on the correspondent's admiration for Richard Beeching, ex-chairman of the British Railways Board, who had proposed to make the railways self-supporting by closing down the unprofitable lines, whatever the cost to passengers and interested workers:

The Rector is applying his techniques with Beechingesque ruthlessness. "I had three churches when I took over the parish and I did not need two," he says. "I knocked one down and converted the other into a hall."

When he was in need of money, which those controlling certain grants were reluctant to provide, he let it be known through the press that he would do one day's work a week for £1,000 a year, and invited the offer of "one or two directorships." . . . His jet-age religion is unlikely to please the traditionalists, who sit worrying, in cloisters far removed from Mayhew's London, that the Cross may be supplanted by Brand X.

Seen from Bermondsey or Woolwich, however, it is a timely anti-
dote to those who have long reacted against the murmur of progress
by singing "Faith of our Fathers"—or its Anglican equivalent—as
loudly as possible. What critics of the South Bank overlook is that
agnostics just can't hear them any longer. I suppose we have got
used to the noise.

If anything, Stacey was a more swashbuckling character than
his admirer made out. There was, for instance, an article by him
in the *Color Magazine* of the *Observer,* titled "A Mission's
Failure: The Story of One Church in Pagan Britain," which was
abundantly illustrated with pictures carrying such captions as
"Stacey broods on parish problems," "The Rector plays the fool
at a social evening for cubs. One only hopes, he says, it is for
Christ's sake," "The Rev. Jeffrey Rowthorn fraternizes with local
children as they leave school. But Sunday-school attendance still
falls," and "Mods and Rockers [note: 'and,' not 'or'] often use
the coffee house in the church's sealed-off galleries." The captions perfectly caught the tone of the article, which read like a
log of ecclesiastical misadventures.

We have been brazen [Stacey wrote] as a Dean Street publicity
agent. In the early stages I pulled a beauty queen on a vegetable
barrow through the main shopping street. . . .
The Bishop of Southwark's mandate to me was: "Build up a team
of clergy and for God's sake do anything to show the people of
Woolwich that the Church exists." . . .
I was chaplain to the Bishop of Birmingham at the time and had
seen many young men accept what bishops delight to call "chal-
lenges" which are really death warrants. It was the newly-appointed
Bishop of Woolwich, Dr. John Robinson, who persuaded me to accept. I had called on him late at night in his suburban home in
Blackheath, having spent hours tramping round the parish. He himself had just come from Clare College, Cambridge, to take on the
job of Bishop of Woolwich and was about as depressed as I was. I
thought it might be interesting to spend the next few years being

depressed about the Church of England together. And so, on the whole, it has proved. . . .

No rector in modern times has had such a team. . . .

Until the *Sun* rose I had a column in the *Daily Herald* for two years, without which we could never have paid the team.

While the team was forming up we rationalised the church buildings. We pulled down one church, after unbelievably complicated legal battles, and turned a terrible little mission church into a hall, now used mainly for Bingo, which, incidentally, has done more to create a community spirit in a slum corner of the parish than anything else we have done. The profits go towards parcels for old people at Christmas.

Our main building task was to transform the enormous Georgian parish church by sealing off the unused galleries and creating a coffee house out of one and a lounge out of the other. In the crypt we put the headquarters of the branch of the Suicide Samaritans.

We came under a barrage of criticism, mainly from outside Woolwich, with the inevitable gibes of "coffee-bar religion." The whole scheme cost £30,000, and since we spent the money before we raised it I nearly landed in prison. . . . For months a gang of the roughest Rockers in town made the Coffee House their evening headquarters. Every day our professional catering staff do more than 60 lunches for shop and office workers. Many people have come from all over the world to see it. But after Princess Margaret and Lord Snowdon had opened it we personally invited every man and woman in the parish—100 at a time—to a Coffee Evening. In spite of the blaze of publicity, only about 5 per cent bothered to turn up—not from hostility, but from an extraordinary lack of curiosity which is a feature of this type of area. . . .

The parents may not understand (who does?) the theology of christening, but our hope has been that they are left with an impression that something really important has happened to their baby. A few days after the christening we call again with a plush christening card, and every year for the five subsequent years a member of the congregation calls with a card on the anniversary of the christening. In spite of all this only one lot of parents from the hundreds of babies we have christened are now church members. . . .

The fact that considerable numbers of parishioners do come to see us with their problems is partly due to the image we have succeeded in creating by taking our public relations seriously. . . . The theological strip-tease act—represented, for instance, by the Bishop of Woolwich's "Honest to God"—is already in progress. . . . But I suspect that we, and perhaps the Church too, have more to learn from our failure than we would have done had we in fact been successful.

Journals that were seriously interested in theology, like the Anglican monthly *Prism,* were forced to take notice of these stunts, though their view of the religious acrobatics promoted by the basically agnostic newspapers was naturally quite different, as when the Reverend Eric James wrote in *Prism* about "A Mission's Failure: The Story of One Church in Pagan Britain":

He [Stacey] makes the statement that at Woolwich they had "one of the largest and ablest teams of clergy of any parish in England." I do not doubt this. . . . But when he begins to give his estimate of their ability I am . . . surprised. It is so dominated by things that are almost irrelevant where love of God, ability to get alongside ordinary people, and concern for humanity are the primary need: ". . . top scholarship from Eton to Trinity, Oxford . . . two Firsts at Cambridge and scholarships to Teheran and New York University." . . .
I thought I knew Nick fairly well, but it never occurred to me that he was still thinking that the central object of the exercise is to get people to come to church. . . . I have no doubt there will be a harvest—but *not* in terms of immediate churchgoing. In my judgment that's just the way to make sure the harvest fails.

In any event, Stacey's article was deemed to have caused such a stir that the B.B.C. decided to devote to it a weekly television program on religion called "Meeting Point." For the purpose, a producer named Peter Ferres, a narrator named James Mitchell (the publisher of the various volumes of "Objections"—"Objections to Christian Belief," "Objections to Roman Catholicism," and "Objections to Humanism"—and the instigator of the last

two), and a camera crew had spent the week in Woolwich inter-
viewing Stacey and his parishioners for a nine-minute film,
which would open the program and then, along with Stacey's article, form the subject of a discussion by Stacey, James, the Bishop
of Southwark, and Mitchell, with Robert McKenzie, B.B.C.'s star
commentator on hot issues, in the moderator's chair. They were
preparing to record the discussion at the time I was in London,
and when I was told that I could sit in on the rehearsal and
recording, which were going to take several hours, and talk with
the participants individually in the course of the day, I made
my way to the B.B.C.'s riverside studios in Hammersmith, where
the session was to be held. At the studio, I was taken in hand
by Ferres, a young Canadian, and introduced to the participants,
all of whom were already there and were being incessantly
moved about by the camera crew, like chess pieces, over and
around the floor, which was covered with heavy cables. I exchanged a few words with, in turn, the Bishop of Southwark,
whose tone of voice alternated unnervingly between the
holy and the stern; Robert McKenzie, who looked rather
sleepy, as though he had been broadcasting a close by-election
all night; Stacey, who had a quick, flashy manner of a type I had
met at Oxford when I was myself an undergraduate there;
Mitchell, a rather nervous man, who looked older than his
twenty-six years; and James, who came through as a very serious
and soulful cleric. Ferres then led me up a catwalk to a crowded
control room overlooking the studio, and, between issuing instructions (over an intercom) to the participants on the floor and
to two engineers and a secretary who were in the control room
with us, explained to me that a free-ranging discussion that was
going on among the participants right at that moment would
both enable the crew to take voice levels and give the members
of the group below a chance to feel at ease with each other,
since even to old friends, as they were, the presence of a bishop
was always a little constraining. "In the recording itself, the dis-

cussion that will immediately follow the Woolwich film will also be a spontaneous one," he continued. "First, the Bishop will be questioned by McKenzie for three or four minutes. Then Mc-Kenzie will ask questions of the other participants. Then there will be a group discussion. The reason for this arrangement is that I want the Bishop to take a stand on Nick's *Observer* article—say Stacey was either right or wrong. At the end, each will sum up in a sentence, so that the viewer is left with some impression of what he has gained from the broadcast." Ferres interrupted himself to call out over the intercom that it was time for a break, and that everyone should adjourn to the Hospitality Room for a snack and a drink.

In the Hospitality Room, there was considerable forced jollity, for it was discovered that the B.B.C. had neglected to lay in any gin, and a page had to be dispatched to a nearby pub to get a bottle. Only James, who was standing in a corner by himself, seemed not to be sharing in the mirth. I went up to him, and he said, "Getting McKenzie is a great compliment to Mervyn and Nick. Peter Ferres told me that they got McKenzie because they didn't want Mervyn to get away with anything. Ferres told McKenzie to pin the Bishop down. The Bishop has a tendency to talk a lot of blah. I drove up with him from his house. Mervyn is worried. You see, he has over five hundred clergy under him, and most of them are very conservative. To them he is Father in God, and he can't afford to upset them. He has a built-in eye for p.r. In Cambridge, he was a brilliant vicar of Great St. Mary's, because he was a kind of impresario. He knew the things that people wanted to discuss, and he had just that extra bit of raffishness. Instead of merely preaching on mundane matters, he would choose the subject of the hour; when the Wolfenden Report on homosexuality came out, in 1957, he preached on that. And so he put the place on the map, much in the way he put Woolwich and Southwark on the map twelve years later. And he is the one who brought me to Southwark.

My first vicarage—my first living, as they call it—was in a church that was built in 1884 and could seat seventeen hundred. When I started there, I had a congregation of thirty-five. I shocked some of my congregation by saying in my first sermon that I would be glad if the building burned down that evening. The sermon was misunderstood, but much of my time in those first weeks was spent trying to find money to repair the hole in the roof, and that kind of thing. If the building had burned down, perhaps the members of the congregation would have come closer to each other."

The Bishop, a tall, imposing man, came up with a plate of sandwiches. "Have a sandwich," he said to me. He had a stentorian voice.

I said I had a question or two for him, if he could spare a few minutes.

"Carry on!" he replied, like a headmaster.

I asked him whether in *his* opinion there was such a thing as South Bank religion.

"The South Bank heresy," he said wryly. "A lot of nonsense has been written about the South Bank. Newspapers have been full of lies about the South Bank. They have made out that there is a South Bank-Cambridge axis, and that everyone in Southwark is a heretic or a fellow-traveller or a Socialist. There is a vicar in my diocese who quarrelled with everybody—Tories, Catholics, Nonconformists. I refused to go to his Communion service. The gutter press headlined it, 'SOCIALIST BISHOP REFUSES TO GO TO TORY'S COMMUNION.' The diocese is a tremendous mixture. There is what I call the gin-and-Jaguar belt, and then there are the slums. I have about three hundred parishes in my diocese, and more than five hundred clergy. Most of these people are ordinary, simple ministers, who spend their day looking after their parishioners. There will be twenty people sick and a certain number of old people whom the minister will have to care for. But the Church is nothing without power; achieving that, too, is Our Lord's work. Had Gordon Walker won the by-election, he would have influence today and be a force for good, but without winning the election where is he today? There is a parish in my diocese that has a congregation of twenty-six. I went to a service there the other day, and I was bored, bored, bored. Yet if God were giving marks for holiness, the minister would certainly get better marks than anyone else I know. He is in the worst and poorest parish. I have tried to offer him better parishes, but he has always refused them. He says that he doesn't mind spending the rest of his life in this parish. There is another vicar, in the same parish, who is, to look at, very unattractive. He blinks, and that kind of thing. But he has personality—that imponderable. What makes a man tick. He has no trouble in getting a congregation of two hundred to three hundred people. One is holier than the other, and he is completely unsuccessful. The other is not holy, and he is successful. Maybe one day we will lose all our power. It may be that all of Europe will go Communist, and England, too, as Marx said, and our buildings will all be taken over. Then the Church will really come up against it. But that might even be a good thing, as far as the life of religion is concerned." As though he had suddenly realized that his remarks might have been a little ambiguous, he started quoting a passage from the Bible story: "'And being in Bethany, in the house of Simon the leper, as he sat at meat, there came a woman having an alabaster box of ointment of spikenard very precious; and she brake the box, and poured it on his head. And there were some that had indignation within themselves, and said, Why was this waste of the ointment made? For it might have been sold for more than three hundred pence, and have been given to the poor. And they murmured against her. And Jesus said, Let her alone; why trouble ye her? she hath wrought a good work on me. For ye have the poor with you always, and whensoever ye will ye may do them good: but me ye have not always.'" He finished, "So, you see, a man may take his wife for

an expensive dinner with a bottle of wine to celebrate his wedding anniversary, though his neighbors are poor and go hungry,
and yet some good things may come out of that dinner and
bottle of wine. Therefore, it is good and necessary."

Ferres made a last round, to press more sandwiches and drinks
on the guests, who had eaten and drunk sparingly. Not having
any success, he shepherded them away, "to have the shine taken
off your noses and foreheads with powder and makeup," as he
put it.

A little later, I found myself reading a sheet of paper. It was
headed:

BATTERSEA PARISH CHURCH

LONDON'S GEORGIAN CHURCH BY THE RIVER

BISHOP OF SOUTHWARK'S VISITATION

It read:

Thursday . . .

6 P.M. The Bishop arrives at Battersea Parish Church to the ringing
of the bells and is received by the Churchwardens.

Legal Visitation Matters.

6:20 P.M. Evening Prayer in the Parish Church.

6:34 P.M. Buffet supper at the "Old Swan."

7:15 P.M. The Bishop will speak to the Parish Youth Council (in
the Edward Wilson Room at the Vicarage).

8 P.M. The Bishop takes the chair of the monthly meeting of the
Church Council (in the Edward Wilson Room).

9 P.M. The Bishop takes prayers with the Rangers and Girl Guides
(in the Hall at the back of the Vicarage).

9:30 P.M. The Bishop takes prayers with the Sea Cadets in the HQ.
(The Parish Church provides the chaplaincy for both the Sea Cadets
and the Air Training Corps.)

The sheet went on to list the agenda for the following day,
calculated to the minute from 7:30 A.M. until 9 P.M., during
which time the Bishop was to call on, meet, pray with, take re-
freshments with, or speak to such groups, individuals, and in-

stitutions as the Katherine Low Settlement, Sir Walter St. John's School, St. Mary's Primary School, Battersea Bridge Buildings, Caius House's Old People's Dinners, the Morgan Crucible Co., Ltd., Councillor S. Sporle, Confirmation candidates, and church-wardens.

Back in the control room with Ferres, I found the participants assembled below, and at a signal from Ferres the Woolwich film went up on the screen in the studio. The film opened with Mitchell talking over the strains of some nondescript music: "Just off this High Street of Woolwich is this bustling market center. Behind me, porticoed and peeling, is the symbol of one revolution—an abandoned cinema. Over here, behind the bill-boards, is the symbol of another revolution—the site of an abandoned church." He went on to summarize Stacey's article. There followed interviews with ten parishioners, which estab-lished that they had no objection to working on Stacey's com-munity projects but, equally, had no interest in going to his church or to any church. One, who spoke for all of them, said, "People who don't go to church can be just as good a Christian as those that do."

Then Stacey appeared, and, in his Oxford stammer, mostly rephrased the contentions of his *Observer* article: "It was five years ago that the Bishop of Southwark asked me to become Rector of St. Mary's Parish, Woolwich. St. Mary's is a typical industrial parish. A parish similar to many others throughout England where the Church is making very little impact. We've been able to sharpen up the services, make them easy to under-stand, to make them brighter. And I think, too, we've been able to create a better image for the Church. As a result of this fairly hard, energetic—I hope, loving—work over the last five years, the congregation has only increased from fifty to a hundred and the number of Confirmation candidates has actually gone down. Well, now, in most industrial parishes, it is clear that the Church is failing because the Church hasn't got the tools for the job. We have had, and we have got, tools for the job but nevertheless we have failed, in churchgoing terms. And my experience is that, apart from certain parishes in the industrial north where there is still more residual Christianity, there's a massive failure by the Church of England in our industrial areas, and the first thing we've got to do is to face this failure before we're going to get a radical renewal of the Church."

The film over, McKenzie immediately opened the discussion in the studio. He began, "Here with me is the man who inspired the project in the first place, the Bishop of Southwark, the Reverend Mervyn Stockwood. Bishop, what exactly—what did you have in mind as an objective in this operation when you first sponsored it?"

"I want to go back to what is the purpose of the Church," the Bishop said. "As I understand it, the Church exists to carry on the work which Jesus had started. What is this work? Well, Jesus was quite secure about this. It is to make the world His kingdom. Thy kingdom come, Thy will be done on earth as it is in Heaven. That is to say, to make all the conditions of this world, and the people, what God wants them to be. Now, He left behind, then, His Church, this body of people to carry on this work. It spread from Jerusalem, from one country to another, and eventually came to England, and it's gone on here for hundreds and hundreds of years. Now, wherever it may be, whether it's in Cheltenham or Woolwich, it makes no difference, it's just for this purpose—to make the world, to make the place where the Church is set, where these people actually live, what God wants them to be. Thy kingdom come, Thy will be done on earth as it is in Heaven. So, when Nick Stacey came to Woolwich, those were the 'marching orders' as they had to be and they always are for any parson. I'd like to—ought to—make it clear. He had no orders different from any other parson that I have in my diocese, which is simply: 'Go ahead and remember that you are Christ's instrument for furthering His kingdom and doing His will.'"

McKenzie tried to make his second question a little more exact. "Now, how far do you accept his own judgment of the five years of work—'that it is a failure, in Church terms'?" he asked.

"Well, I don't really think that I'm qualified," the Bishop said, and added, with authority, "I'm not sure that he's qualified, to pass judgment on these things." He went on, seemingly returning to some script on the lectern in his mind, "You see, one has to judge the Church by the impact it makes upon the world in which it's set. Let me put it like this. A young man comes to me and says, 'Bishop, I want to be ordained now. I'm thinking of going to St. Wilfred's. Tell me, is there strong churchmanship at St. Wilfred's?' And I say, 'Well, look here, my boy, what can . . . I mean, are you asking me, What is the candlepower of St. Wilfred's? Or are you asking me, What is the impact it makes upon the locality?' Now, that is how I judge the strength or weakness of the Church. You see, you make an impact in two ways. First, the Church as a community, on the borough council, the trade unions, employer federations—on public opinion. For instance, is the Church really making an impact on anything like racial feeling? On approaches to education?"

McKenzie cut the Bishop short and tried once again to make him focus on the original question: "But does this mean, Bishop, you don't accept the criterion that it seems to me Stacey was applying in the latter part of his statement—namely, that unless you can bring people into religious worship in the Church, you really can't claim to have succeeded?"

The Bishop persisted. "No, I don't judge that—judge it in that way. As I said, I judge it by the general impact it makes and also by the personal impact. Let me put it this way. I was talking to one of the mayors the other day, and he said to me, 'I'm not a churchman but since I've been mayor I've been going to church a lot and coming a lot into touch with church people.' He said, 'During the past few months I've been staggered by what I've seen church people doing for the old and the young—running clubs and bothering about people.' He said, 'I really do feel rather ashamed about some of the criticisms that I've made.'" The Bishop suddenly seemed to become aware that perhaps he had carried on his homely filibuster a little too long, and said disarmingly, "Now, I agree that what I have said so far has been concerned with the practical impact of Christianity, but that isn't a bad way of beginning." Here he again cited chapter and verse, as though it were second nature to him. "Didn't Jesus Himself say that you're going to be tested when you die by whether you've fed the hungry and given water to the thirsty and visited the prisoners, and so on?"

McKenzie craftily approached his quarry from another direction. Instead of referring to Stacey's church-attendance argument yet again in terms of the Church's relative "failure," he now tried to make the Bishop evaluate the experiments in terms of their relative "success," saying, "But on this very point. Now, surely, if all that was done—and it may be done very well—was a combination of a citizens' advice bureau, a youth club, a welfare agency, this is surely not, in religious terms, a wholly successful operation?"

But the Bishop was not so easily taken. "It isn't just that," he said. "You see, these things are the fruit of one's deep convictions. Now, lots of things that happen in church bore me, and I could criticize them as much as anybody else. But, nevertheless, I am a believer in church services. I mean, I have three services every day in my chapel. At Bishop's House I get Communion nearly every day of my life. I do believe in church services."

McKenzie tried still another gambit. "But why does it not

attract people?" he said. "We've heard people in the film saying that while we like helping Stacey's project here we just don't go to church."

The Bishop beat a deceptive retreat: "Because I think they don't understand it. I think the whole sort of setup of our church is frightfully difficult for the man in the street to come to grips with."

"But then don't you have to change—" McKenzie began plaintively.

The Bishop did not allow him to finish. Instead, he went on to shore up his own new position, this time with history. "Ah," he said. "I think the Church of England is so—so stern-looking, people don't think . . . You see, this is where I disagree with . . . I think it was— Was it James Mitchell who said in that film that people have left the Church? You see, the working classes have never belonged to it. It was the tradespeople who lived there. We have the— I mean the evidence of previous surveys in London at the beginning of the century. The position today is really no different from what it was then, it was just the tradespeople and middle-class people who went there."

"Bishop, I—" McKenzie tried to break in.

"And I couldn't agree with you more," the Bishop said. "I think that the whole sort of setup of the Church—its priorities, its values, its absurd and fantastic legalism, which cripples most reforms—is part of the reason why people simply cannot break through and understand what they're about."

The Bishop had gone over his time, and McKenzie said, "May I come back to you in a moment, Bishop?" He went on, "Now, the man who was involved in this project—right on the ground, as it were—Nicolas Stacey. Stacey, listening to the Bishop's observations on the whole operation, would you be inclined to, in any way, modify your word 'failure'?"

"No, I wouldn't, because, you see, I think the Bishop has ducked the issue," Stacey replied. "The Church has traditionally taught that man is a worshipping animal, the Church is structured on the basis that worship is important. We maintain, I think, twenty thousand Anglican places of worship in England and Wales. In our services—our Baptism service, for instance, we get the parents and godparents to promise that they'll bring their children to be confirmed, i.e., go to church when they're the right age. The whole Church is structured on the basis that worship is important, and I wanted to show to the Church that in worship, in churchgoing terms, we're failing."

McKenzie said, "Next, James Mitchell, who did a survey on the ground, as you saw in the Woolwich film—himself an Anglican layman. Mitchell, you talked to the people down there in the course of this survey. Do you think Stacey is justified in calling the whole operation a failure?"

"Well, it depends on what terms you call failure," Mitchell said. "In churchgoing terms, obviously this is so."

McKenzie, adroit moderator that he was, repeated perhaps the only concrete defense he had managed to extract from the Bishop: "But the Bishop's point was that the working class—and this, after all, is a primary working-class area—has not since the Industrial Revolution been in the Church."

"That's quite true," Mitchell agreed. "But, on the other hand, the middle classes are now leaving the Church, whereas perhaps in the past they never did. But I think really the whole criterion of churchgoing as a measure is no longer valid. You see, both the Bishop and Stacey have been talking in words like 'worship,' 'impact,' and 'image,' and every time a word like this is mentioned I always feel somehow behind it all there's a kind of self-deception." Mitchell, too, seemed to have prepared an argument in advance, and now he aired it: "I think the great menace of Christianity, as a religion, is that it gives people socially respectable excuses for really exercising their own vanity or power. I think that a lot of the concern in the Church at the moment about churchgoing—and, indeed, the impact of the Church, as the Church people now have been talking—may be disguised anxiety about the fact that they haven't any longer got people in their power."

"Well, now another priest, who's dealt with a similar kind of situation," McKenzie said. "The Reverend Eric James, who is the director of Parish and People and who has a parish in southeast London as well. What's your feeling, having dealt with the same sort of problem?"

"Well, there's so much to comment on here," James said. "Just picking up one of the random statements . . . I feel that if one just says that churchgoing and belonging to the Church is an excuse for people's vanity, that really is trivial, as a comment." The program, never quite under control, suddenly went off the deep end. "Because if you've known and loved and worked with people in your parish, you know how many of your worshippers are sustained in looking after their husbands. I think of my . . . one person in my mind, looking after her husband when he's got cancer and arthritis and so on. Devoted—a conservative in my mind, religiously, and disagreeing very much with the kind of thing I had to do, and yet devoted and humble and sustained by their worship. Nevertheless, to get to the main point, I would say that I agree entirely with Mr. Stacey's judgment that, in churchgoing terms, the work of the Church is a failure at the moment. And I believe, certainly, that the Church must not be judged on whether people come to church. I believe this is a wrong criterion. I think—"

"What is the right one?" McKenzie broke in.

"I think that I would want to see the Church geared—very much, at the moment—to helping people live at depth," James said. "A bishop said to me the other day, 'The trouble at the moment is that life only helps people to live their lives at a chatty level.' Now, I believe the Church has got to help people to live deeply human lives. One of the most marvellous things that Pilate said, sort of inadvertently, about Jesus was 'Behold the man.'

Now, people ought to be able to say of Christians 'Behold the man,' and they ought to be able to say of the Church that everything that goes on in it is helping them to become human, deeply human. I would agree that so often what the Church is doing is helping people to follow a kind of centuries-old cultus which has little relevance to being deeply human. But we've got to help people to be human and to live in community."

Some time later, McKenzie said to Stacey, "Now, you've been criticized by some for having been in your article, and perhaps even in your statement now, defeatist and negative; what do you see as the way out as someone who presumably is still committed to the Church?"

"I don't know what the way out is," Stacey replied. "I think we've got to the point at which I feel that no longer will the traditional, orthodox method ever work. I think we're going to see a stripping down of the Church, that it will cease to be a great estate of the realm, we shall have far fewer church buildings, most clergymen will be earning their living in secular activities, and I think the Church will develop in little cells of people meeting in each other's houses and trying to discuss and pray together and only very rarely, perhaps, come to places of worship for great services, and they will be concerned not to run ecclesiastical organizations and ecclesiastical structures but to be in the secular ones."

"Bishop," McKenzie said, "this is a pretty drastic diagnosis of what happens next. How far would you go along with it?"

The Bishop did a complete about-face, and became almost indistinguishable from the critics of his earlier position. "I'd go a long way with that," he said. "I'm perfectly prepared to get rid of most of our buildings. I could get rid of about fifty per cent of them in my diocese; it would be a great help to the spread of Christianity, I think, if we could. And, once we have done that, to concentrate on the fact that we are not just individual Christians, we are members of a community. The only service, really,

I want them to get to at all is the Communion, because there you see a symbol of everything a Christian should be doing. That is that we gather around a table, we take the things of this earth, bread and wine—what we have we have in common. There's no rank, no precedence, no color."

When I came down from the control room after the program, I found James and Stacey sitting by the front door. They said they were waiting for a taxi, which they were going to share. Stacey, on his way to Woolwich, was going to drop James at his home, in Dulwich. The Bishop, McKenzie, and Mitchell had already left.

"I honestly think that you said you were disappointed about the failure so that you could write a good story for the *Observer*," James said. "You couldn't ever have thought, Nick, that all those things would raise church attendance. I thought to myself when I read the article that to expect that from your labors you must be either very conservative or ignorant."

Stacey was silent.

I asked Stacey, "And what did you think of the Bishop's remark that the working classes had never been churchgoers, that surveys taken in the last century show that?"

"In spite of the sociological factor, I believed that with a staff and church program such as we have at Woolwich we could get a breakthrough in churchgoing terms," Stacey said. "I have been proved wrong."

James said to me, "The Bishop did say that he wouldn't mind getting rid of fifty per cent of the church buildings in Southwark."

"But as long as he doesn't say which buildings, then his clergy needn't take offense at it," Stacey said. "I don't think the program got off the ground."

Most of the theologians I met in England acknowledged at one time or another that the Achilles' heel of their calling might be a lack of extended training in philosophy, admitting that their reasoning powers were not always up to defending their faith, and this at a time when most theologians wished to have a reasoned faith and to be able to conduct a dialogue with agnostics and rationalists. I was eager to meet the Reverend Canon Ian T. Ramsey, Nolloth Professor of the Philosophy of the Christian Religion at Oxford, and no relation of the Archbishop, because, among the new theologians, he was a splendid exception. He had once said of himself, "I am an odd man out. I went to Cambridge and read mathematics, and switched over to philosophy, which is called Moral Sciences there. Then I took up theology. Because of coming from these scientific and philosophical and theological directions, I find there is no one with me in all my paths. For instance, when I am talking to philosophers I have scientists and theologians in mind, which, normally, the philosophers I'm talking to haven't got in mind. And theologians do not always appreciate the difficulties of a philosopher. And when you come to the scientists, you've got so much of theology and philosophy to represent to *them*. One feels a certain loneliness in this work. One never feels embedded in a community. It's not that people aren't friendly and aren't interested, but you do feel rather a lonely fellow."

For all his scientific and philosophical and theological directions, Ian Ramsey didn't quite enjoy among the students of these separate disciplines the fearful status of a cat among pigeons, precisely because his diverse interests, and the questions and answers arising out of them, were not quite comprehensible, or even interesting, to those whose training had been in just one of these disciplines. Yet Ramsey was now embedded primarily in the community of theologians, and one felt that if any theologian was free from the charge of philosophical confusion it must be he. His books were, in fact, notable for an effort to put a scientific scaffolding under the theological language, as when, in "Models and Mystery," he expounded the terms central to his thesis—"models," "qualifiers," and "disclosures."

Theology (I would say) is founded in occasions of insight and disclosure when, to put it at its most general, the universe declares itself in a particular way around some group of events which thus take on a cosmic significance [he wrote]. These events then become, and naturally, a self-appointed model which enables us to be articulate about what has been disclosed. But no more here than elsewhere is the model to be a scale or pictorial model, and here it is more than ever essential to register and emphasize the logical gap between the model and what the insight reveals, between the model and the situation in which it is fulfilled. . . . Let us approach the matter thus. So important is logical diversification for theology that, lest we should be tempted to rely on one model alone, theology provides built-in stimuli for the never-ending development of any model. This is effected by words we may call "qualifiers." The intention is to produce, from a single model, and by means of some qualifier, an endless series of variants, between any pair of which there will occur implicit metaphors, in this way witnessing to the fact that the heart of theology is permanent mystery. Here is the function in theology of words like "infinite," "perfect," "all"—such words we call "qualifiers"—words which multiply models without end and with subtle changes, creating in this way what might be called, following Wittgenstein, models with family resemblances, a family of models. So a qualifier like "infinite" will work on a model of human love until there dawns on us that particular kind of family resemblance between the various derivative models which reveals God—God as "infinitely loving." God is revealed in the cosmic disclosure which may occur at some stage as the pattern of models is developed without end, just as there may dawn on us that to which an infinite convergent series points, as its terms are endlessly developed. Qualifiers thus provide not only for the endless construction of metaphors; they are at the same time the words in theology that witness to its grounding in permanent mystery, that point to a cosmic disclosure as that alone which reveals the topic of any and every theological utterance.

So in theology it is not only that a model permits of articulation. In theology the model must occur in a phrase which incorporates also a qualifier which in its simplest form will be a word or a suffix designed to make sure that here the main point of the model is seen to be its fulfillment in a disclosure. At every stage in theological reasoning the route from a model to a mystery must be indicated. All that is not to deny the possibility of progressive understanding— far from it. It is merely a matter of where the essential emphasis is to be placed, and in theology the emphasis must be unambiguously on the disclosure basis of its utterances.

Ramsey, whom I recently met one day for lunch in his rooms at Oriel College, turned out to be a short, stoutish, vigorous north-countryman. He seemed impatient to get onto a discussion of theology, so, over sherry, I asked him about his theory of models and disclosures.

He said, "Very crudely, and forgetting the complexities of the theory of inferior models, I would define a model simply like this: A model is any kind of picture or example on which people can agree and by which they can be led to understand something of which at present they are not certain or about which they are perplexed. There are obvious similarities with, say, the model ship that a boy will provide to understand what the great boat is like. Or perhaps an airplane is better, if I just don't know what a Viscount X is like. As for disclosures, I'll use an example of a polygon to illuminate basically what I mean by that. The point would be: Suppose we are invited to draw a number of regular polygons with an increasing number of sides, all their vertices to be equidistant from a fixed point. We then draw on a blackboard, say, a square, a pentagon, a hexagon, a heptagon, and so on. And we might say after doing—I don't know—say, thirty of these, 'What do you see?' Now, the plain man will always say, 'Thirty polygons,' and, of course, he is obviously right. But the hope is that at some point or other a person might be struck by something when the polygons were developed in this way—he might 'see' something else—namely, a circle. Now, that's what I mean by a disclosure, and I should have thought that for a religious disclosure some stories would have to be told about wisdom or love or power, or something like this, so that you would get feelings of instances making up a pattern, so that sometime or other a disclosure would break in on you. And if this disclosure case involves—the polygon case doesn't—in some way the whole universe, then I call it a cosmic disclosure, and I think one could say that that discloses God. Now, to the question 'What *sort* of God is this?' and so on, I would say at once that if we said that the cosmic disclosure disclosed God, we couldn't say more about God than the models entitled us to speak of, which brings me back to this question of models. If, for instance, at some point or other, one had been challenged by a love of this cosmic kind—as the old hymn would say, 'Love so amazing, so divine, demands my soul, my life, my all,' and so on—one would then say that if one wished to say that one had known God in this disclosure, one would have to picture God in terms of love, which this model has suggested. There are other models—of power, and wisdom, and many other things—and if one claimed that God was disclosed in each case, again one would have to picture God in terms of the language one can best build up from all the models together."

"Would you then also say that all language has models?" I asked.

"I think that far more of our language than we realize is characterized by this feature," he replied. "Certainly all theological language trades in models. And models and disclosures—my key ideas—I try to some extent to develop in relation to the arguments for God's existence, the problem of evil, the concept of miracle, and so on. I use these ideas to reinterpret traditional problems. I see my theory as a more generalized form of Aquinas's doctrine of analogy, but it depends less than his did on a kind of background metaphysics. For instance, you couldn't justify St. Thomas's doctrine of analogy unless, as part of your metaphysical background, you adopted his theory of the Creation, which is, roughly, that since God created the world of man, there is a kind of common background between them. So that words used by men, of men, must have some kind of relation to God, because the Creation has given God and man a kind of common link. But I myself simply try to describe the Creation in terms of these models. I would say the Creation is the way of understanding a certain kind of cosmic disclosure, which can come to us when we ask ourselves the question 'Why is there anything at all?' This question brings up certain patterns, which we reflect on, and then at some point or other we get a feeling of cosmological dependence. That would be my basis for adopting a theory of the Creation. But I wouldn't put this theory in a sacrosanct position. I think it would have to be justified in relation to a disclosure reached in a particular way."

In spite of his neat and precise elaboration, Ian Ramsey seemed to me to leave out the old, intractable question of objectivity—to put it one way, just because one has an idea (that is, a disclosure) of God, does such a God necessarily exist in actuality? I asked, "Even granting that there may be disclosures, does that mean that there is anything objective to correspond to them?"

"Certainly. Disclosures might be objective in the classical sense, in the way that one would start with things like tables and chairs and trees and melons, or whatever it happened to be, and try to move from the existence of present objects to God," Ramsey said. "In such a case, the models would be tables and chairs and trees, but, of course, models for God might be anything. But what I would prefer to say is that God is objective in the sense in which, when we are aware of ourselves, we are always aware of something *other* than ourselves—in the universe, that is."

"But what if someone were to argue—indeed, people have argued—that 'I am not aware of this "other" '?" I asked.

"My next move would be to say that in some way they haven't

been aware of themselves, in my sense, and that they have to re-create that self-awareness, that awareness of their subjectivity, and have to give themselves some kind of self-affirmation," he replied. "Any situation in which they did, in this sense, affirm themselves would be a situation in which they would affirm themselves in relation to something else. One would affirm oneself in the face of some moral challenge, for instance. So I think the objectivity of God is best known as being that which we discern other than ourselves in some self-affirmation like this."

"This 'other' seems to have shifted in meaning. Does it refer to a person, a thing, a challenge, or what?" I asked.

"It could be all of them—anything," he replied. "I mean, one could obviously have this cosmic disclosure through friends, and some religious people have spoken of seeing God in their friends. One could have it through chairs and tables, as when we speak of them as part of the created world. One might even have routes to God through dream images; the Bible is full of passages where people do relate dream images to God's activity. I have God immanent in the technical sense, but I should say my transcendence of God is safeguarded because of the mystery of these cosmic disclosures—models never capture them entirely. There's always a fringe to the cosmic disclosure which we haven't yet grasped in our concept, and so on. God is transcendent in this sense, but also God is transcendent as we transcend our visible behavior. We meet God, as it were, in a mutual participation. In being aware of ourselves as active, we are aware of God's activity challenging us through our friends, chairs, tables, and so on. Well, the God who meets us there is obviously more than that which we see. You see, I am conscious of wanting to use the word 'God' in a much more traditional sense than Tillich and others do. I would use the word 'God' rather than 'depth' or 'the unconditional,' for instance."

Through the window floated the regular tolling of college bells and the irregular click of wooden bowls and the sudden shouts, the laughter, and the mannered accents of undergraduates passing below. Ramsey's own accent was rugged and distinctive (he pronounced "miracle" as if it were spelled "merkel"), and once or twice I thought of asking him where in the North he was from, but it was difficult to break into his flow, even with questions about models and disclosures—questions I found myself asking more and more in the manner of those celebrated but essentially anonymous guests at Plato's Greek feasts whose presence seemed to be justified only by their occasionally asking a question that kept Socrates talking. During a toy banquet—melon, lamb curry, rice, and Major Grey's chutney, followed by fresh strawberries, served almost invisibly by an old-fashioned servant of the college who might easily have come out of "Zuleika Dobson"—I found myself turning, reluctantly, to what could perhaps be called the crystal-ball aspect of Ramsey's theory. I had read that his concept of models and disclosures was so inclusive that it solved even the problem of what would happen to traditional morality, not to mention the Bible, in a future society, such as the one described in "1984," in which people might be controlled like automata through tampering with their genes and glands. I asked him about this now.

"If one day some persons mechanically controlled the beliefs and decisions of others, moral problems would arise, for one, around the persons who were manipulating other people's behavior," he said affably. "They could always ask themselves, if no one else did, 'Is it right for us to be doing this to these other people?' For another, just because certain behavior becomes mechanical need not mean that all moral situations disappear. The very first time I tied a white tie for a dinner, it took a tremendous amount of deliberate activity. I had to follow the rules of tying a tie—putting the tie in and round and underneath, and so on. I know this wasn't a very moral situation particularly; it was a kind of primitive behavior pattern. Well, after doing this for years one does it automatically. One doesn't bother reading anything on tying a tie, and the challenge, that of tying this tie, has been absorbed in my routine and become almost mechanistic behavior. But because I've now no time to waste on tying ties, I can, I hope, make myself available for much more challenging decisions and problems. So I think I could 'save morality' in a society like that of '1984' by doing my best to discover what would be new moral situations in those new circumstances. My theory is, you see, that, at the very least, those persons in control would realize their subjectivity, their self-affirmation, since man is more than all the models I have spoken about—more, because these models are only third-person terms. It seems to me that there will always be the possibility—no matter how far modern biology might go, no matter how far cybernetics might go, no matter how far psychiatry might go, and so on—of disclosing to each of us our subjectivity, because all these scientific disciplines are third-person in character, whereas our subjectivity, in the sense of that self-affirmation, is a first-person assertion. There will always be certain occasions when a first-person utterance, like 'I'm running'—belonging to our self-affirmation—is logically different from any number of third-person assertions, like 'He's running,' into which it could be unpacked. A first-person utterance can never—logically, never—be reduced to a third-person utterance. But I can see some cases in a future society where there will be no actual difference—no difference that would amount to anything—between first- and third-person assertions, between 'I'm running' and 'He's running.' In that future society, I may be running like a machine—I may have been drugged; I may even react against what I am doing, but my legs will be going round, my breath will be coming out, my arms will be moving, I will be running mechanically. Indeed, there may be no actual difference at this moment between your saying 'Ramsey's over there' and my saying 'I'm over here.' But I would still want to maintain that the latter is a significant first-person utterance, since, as I said, I want to maintain that man is more than the models, that he has that subjectivity. Now, it is possible that occasions for our self-affirmation may shrink in number in some future time. It may well be that our particular present occasions for this self-affirmation will have disappeared altogether. But even if the old instances, like the case of my tying my tie, had disappeared forever, I'd have hope that in that new environment new chances of self-affirmation would arise. I am going to be quite fantastic now, of course, but, supposing that we were all organized in such a way everywhere as to be matched up in marriage to the right partner—you know, this is something that is utterly fantastic—there would be new occasions in that situation for affirming our personalities in ways we don't now do. I mean, obviously, that in that particular area of choosing a partner the chances of self-affirmation would have been lost. But I should hope that in that new civilization there would be many more new chances—unfortunately, I haven't the imagination to suppose what they'd be—that would require us to take a new look altogether at our behavior. It might be a fantastically different civilization, in which moral problems would arise not around marriage and the home but around travelling to Mars in three days."

"Even if somehow a place were found for morality in such an unimaginably different civilization, would this morality have anything to do with the Bible, which is, after all, the basis of Christianity?" I asked.

"For me the Bible does present, through its images, its models, its parables, and so on—it does present what I call this cosmic disclosure," Ramsey said. "Now, the real problem that would arise in that civilization is the one that arose even in the first centuries of the Christian era—how to interpret this impact of Jesus of Nazareth, the Christ, in terms of contemporary culture and behavior. Now, what we have in the Bible, you see, is a record—a translation—of that impact in, very broadly, first- and second-century terms. And in central Church doctrines we have the translation of that impact into terms extending over, say, the first five centuries. Now, what sermons ought to do—I don't say what they always do do, but what they ought to do in principle— is somehow to extend that insight consistently into the very time in which the sermons are being preached. While it would be very difficult for the man in 2068 or 3554, or whatever it's going to be, to read the Bible—which might, of course, have been translated into some entirely different language, and so on—it would not be logically impossible for him to relate this by a very long process to the very thought forms of his own kind."

"But would there be any necessity for this?" I asked.

"The necessity would be, or would arise, only if a man living in that world had somehow found in and through this Bible a challenge to which, in a phrase, he had to respond and could do no other. Otherwise, there would be no point in preaching on it. The existence of such a challenge presupposes, of course, that there had been a continuing community that had year by year been reinterpreting this Bible. In a sermon on the Bible, then, the shepherd, whom we might liken to a personnel manager today, might be likened in that world to a spaceman."

"But if the symbols are being continuously translated in this way, won't the message eventually become so different from the original that it will no longer, in a sense, be the message of the Bible?"

"Yes," Ramsey said. "I ought to make it clear that I am not thinking of complete replacement, of substituting contemporary images, or images of the future, for the Biblical ones. I am thinking more of finding illuminating parallels in present and future society. What I am really suggesting is that somehow, through preaching and interpretation, we have continuously to forge links between the old and the new, between the shepherd and the personnel manager, between the shepherd and the space-man."

"But if a society came into existence in which, say, the sacrifice asked of Abraham seemed irrelevant, or in which, to put it in your terms and in an extreme form, the Bible struck nobody with a cosmic disclosure, what possible role could Christianity have then?" I asked.

"I think then we'd be in a very healthy state, if I may say so, because we'd be in the very state of the early Christians, when, for instance, Logos philosophy had struck men with a cosmic disclosure, and what Christians did, rightly, was to relate that disclosure—the disclosure of natural religion—to Christianity. They produced a thing like the Fourth Gospel, which interpreted Jesus in terms of a contemporary, or what might be called secular, concept—in terms of the Logos. And there have been many people all down the ages who have related, for instance, a disclosure of duty to the disclosure of Jesus. And while I am on cosmic disclosures I would also like to say that there are cosmic disclosures in the Koran, but I wouldn't, of course, want to give the Koran an exclusive place. In other words, I want to have all the cosmic disclosures in the Koran—they are all quite legitimate cosmic disclosures—but at the moment, being a Christian, I think there can be certain claims made for the uniqueness of Jesus, though not a uniqueness that denies significance to everything else. I think this would, of course, have to be argued in terms— Well, I won't go into details now, but in terms such as one finds in the Epistle to the Romans, in the New Testament, about the place of Jesus in the whole pattern of history, and so on. If the claim for Our Lord's uniqueness weren't substantiated in history, then I think it would be less reasonable."

III

PASTOR BONHOEFFER

Next to the late Dietrich Bonhoeffer, Bishop Robinson
relied most heavily for "Honest to God" on Rudolf Bultmann, who was, and is, one of the two preëminent living Protestant theologians on the Continent, the other being his main
adversary, Karl Barth—who has written twelve brilliant volumes
of theology, in his "Church Dogmatics," about the impossibility
both of writing theology and of speculating at all about the
divine nature, so far separated, Barth argued, was man from
God. (Once, Brunner, of Zurich, was thought to be in the same
class, but his star has been in eclipse now for many years.) Some
months ago, I wrote to both of them, in the hope that I might
be able to talk with them, though I knew Barth was touching
eighty, while Bultmann had passed it, and neither one of them
was in very good health. Both wrote to say that they would be
glad to see me. I went first to Basel, where Barth lives and
used to teach, at the University of Basel.

Barth's house, a modest three-story structure, was on Bruder-
holzallee, in the southeast of Basel. The door was answered by
an anxious-looking elderly lady with white hair, who was wearing a blue wool dress. This was Mrs. Barth. *"Guten Tag,"* Mrs.
Barth said. "My husband can't talk very long. He's just come
back from the hospital, where he has been for three months."

She conducted me to the stairs, then paused indecisively at the foot, and took me into a small living room overlooking a withered, wintry garden. She said, "My son-in-law is a landscape architect. He helped design this garden. In summer, this garden will be very nice; there will be flowers. When my husband gets stronger, we will have seminars in the restaurant across the street. His students come there, to discuss and write. That's where he wrote some of the 'Dogmatics.' We rent a room from the restaurant." Hesitating a bit longer, she told me how Barth spent a day when he was teaching and in good health. From her account, he appeared to have led a monk's life. He used to get up a little before seven o'clock; he thought aloud to himself from seven to seven-thirty; from seven-thirty to seven-forty-five he listened to Mozart, his favorite composer, about whom he had written a book; he read and wrote from seven-forty-five until lunch, which, if he was too preoccupied, he missed; at three-forty-five, having worked until the last minute—most of the time on a lecture that later became a chunk in the next volume of the "Dogmatics," the book growing with each such addition, volume by volume, year after year—he left the house for his four-fifteen lecture at the university; and he worked again after the lecture from five-thirty to one or two at night (relying, by day and evening, on the help of his long-time, devoted secretary, Fräulein Charlotte von Kirschbaum, who had studied with him), finishing off with some detective stories, which, with Mozart, gave him his only relaxation. Occasionally, he liked a good bottle of wine or a plate of snails (which he had eaten for the first time five years before). Otherwise, his needs were simple.

Mrs. Barth then led me back to the stairs, which were covered with a worn red carpet. On the wall alongside them were prints of famous philosophers and theologians, ascending from Kant to Schleiermacher to Nitzsch to Neander to Richard Rothe to Blumhardt to Wilhelm Herrmann to Harnack. At the top of the stairs was a rather wasted figure with a strong, pugnacious peasant's face. He had on black-and-white striped trousers and a green wool shirt open at the neck, and he was wearing glasses and smoking a short pipe. This was Barth himself, the pupil of Harnack. Having greeted me warmly, he led the way into a very small and austere room—his study. In the center of the room was a round table, spread with a plain beige cloth. All around were worn gray books, in English, French, German, Latin, Greek, and Hebrew. One shelf, at eye level, held volumes upon volumes of his own works. On another shelf, next to the ceiling, were books written about him. One could just make out a few of the titles: "Karl Barth," "Catholicism and Barthianism," "Portrait of Karl Barth." The two of us sat down at the table.

"I wish you had come five years ago," Barth said. "You would have found another fellow. He would have been quick, but I've just come out of the hospital, and I'm lucky to have any memory at all."

I said that I was grateful for the opportunity to shake his hand, and I went on to say that in the rounds I had been making among the theologians I had discovered two Barths: one the radical Barth who in 1918 had published the revolutionary book "The Epistle to the Romans," which was still constantly read and referred to, and the other the conservative Barth who was known for the "Church Dogmatics," to which he had devoted himself since the late twenties. How did the two manage to get on together?

He laughed, but only for a moment; it seemed a strain. With an effort, he said, "Yes, the commentary on Romans is a radical work, written in my youth. Then I became more tranquil, peaceful, universal-minded, and I wrote the 'Dogmatics.' Most people like the commentary, because it is radical, but the 'Dogmatics' is my more important work—if it is not so much read, it is because people don't take the trouble to read twelve volumes. The commentary is one-sided, but the 'Dogmatics' is many-sided."

I remarked that the late Pope John had compared him and his "Dogmatics" to Aquinas and the "Summa Theologica."

"I didn't know that," Barth said, looking away. He continued, "Dogmatic theology repeats the big yes that God gave the world. God loves the world in which we have to live. We have to say yes to the world. The presupposition of the 'Dogmatics' is that the Gospel is the word of God. Most theologians—most notably Bultmann—begin nowadays with the morals, the ethics of religion, or with man, but the presupposition of all dogmatic theology is that one has to begin with God."

"The God of the New Testament seems very different from that of the Old," I remarked hesitantly.

"The Old Testament is the story of the people of Israel, and this story is a prefiguration of Christ," he said. "Christ is the final revelation. Among the Gospels there are differences, contradictions, but the similarities are far greater, and they have to be kept in mind. The Gospel writers were the witnesses to the word of God."

Barth looked tired, and I felt I should take my leave.

As I got up, he rose and put a hand on my shoulder. "My eldest son, Markus, is in America," he said. "He teaches New Testament theology in the Pittsburgh Theological Seminary. Perhaps you will meet him someday."

Some people see Bultmann as a sort of Atlas, supporting with his doctrine of demythologization the world of radical theology (though Bultmann can easily pass as a theologian in a classical sense, too; it is thought that a work like "Das Evangelium des Johannes" has such exegetical and critical value that it will be read long into the future, regardless of the fate of any one of Bultmann's philosophical ideas). Indeed, it is said that the German Evangelical Church would like to try Bultmann for heresy if a prosecutor could be found who was his match in theology. About the doctrine of demythologization Bultmann has written:

The question inevitably arises: Is it possible that Jesus's preaching of the Kingdom of God still has any importance for modern men and the preaching of the New Testament as a whole is still important for modern men? . . . We must ask whether the eschatological preaching and the mythological sayings as a whole contain a still deeper meaning which is concealed under the cover of mythology. If that is so, let us abandon the mythological conceptions precisely because we want to retain their deeper meaning. This method of interpretation of the New Testament which tries to recover the deeper meaning behind the mythological conceptions I call "de-mythologizing"—an unsatisfactory word, to be sure. Its aim is not to eliminate the mythological statements but to interpret them. It is a method of hermeneutics. . . . According to mythological thinking, God has His domicile in heaven. What is the meaning of this state-ment? The meaning is quite clear. In a crude manner, it expresses the idea that God is beyond the world, that He is transcendent. The thinking which is not yet capable of forming the abstract idea of transcendence expresses its intention in the category of space; the transcendent God is imagined as being at an immense spatial dis-tance, far above the world: for above this world is the world of the stars, of the light which enlightens and makes glad the life of men. When mythological thinking forms the conception of hell, it ex-presses the idea of the transcendence of evil as the tremendous power which again and again afflicts mankind. The location of hell and of men whom hell has seized is below the earth in darkness, because darkness is tremendous and terrible to men. These mythological con-ceptions of heaven and hell are no longer acceptable for modern men, since for scientific thinking to speak of "above" and "below" in the universe has lost all meaning, but the idea of the transcendence of God and of evil is still significant. . . . The eschatological preaching of Jesus was retained and continued by the early Christian com-munity in its mythological form. But very soon the process of demythologizing began, partially with Paul, and radically with John. The decisive step was taken when Paul declared that the turning point from the Old World to the New was not a matter of the future but did take place in the coming of Jesus Christ. . . . An ob-jection often heard against the attempt to demythologize is that it takes the modern world-view as the criterion of the interpretation of the Scripture and the Christian message and that Scripture and Christian message are not allowed to say anything that is in contradiction with the modern world-view. It is, of course, true that demythologizing takes the modern world-view as a criterion. To demythologize is to reject not Scripture or the Christian message as a whole, but the world-view of Scripture, which is the world-view of a past epoch, which all too often is retained in Christian dogmatics and in the preaching of the Church. . . . For the world-view of the Scripture is mythological and is therefore unacceptable to modern man, whose thinking has been shaped by science and is therefore no longer mythological. . . . Now it is the Word of God which calls man into genuine freedom, into free obedience, and the task of demythologizing has no other purpose but to make clear the call of the Word of God. It will interpret the Scripture, asking for the deeper meaning of mythological conceptions and freeing the Word of God from a bygone world-view.

But the more Bultmann has tried to give this doctrine an intellectual basis, the more he has discouraged many Christians with what they consider his essential irrationalism. In conversation with me, Ian Ramsey, a sympathetic critic, had said, "Insofar as Bultmann is saying, Don't think the Gospels are just picture books, exact records of, for instance, what Christ did; they are about something much more telling than this, about a mighty peculiar kind of thing, which might be called 'authentic existence,' or what he calls 'the deeper meaning'—so far he's all right. I think he's also very right when he says that the kind of situation the Gospel is trying to portray is one of metaphysical—theological—significance but nevertheless one in which we are personally very involved. I think he's weak, or inadequate, at any rate, insofar as he tends to minimize the historical elements in the Bible—by taking refuge behind Heidegger, he almost cuts himself off from any possibility of arguing reasonably about this authentic existence. You see, I think that we have to pay more attention than he does to the historical elements and have to establish much better than he does what are more and what are less reliable ways of talking about this authentic existence. But in drawing people away from a mere kind of historicism, I think he is first-rate. And in suggesting that you don't understand the Bible or the New Testament unless there is some kind of personal commitment here—all this is first-rate. But I think he tends to be a bit, in the broad sense of the word, irrational. To despise the historicity arguments, as it were, and to think that whatever can be found out by historical criticism makes no difference—to think of this as of no account, so to say—I think this is irrational."

Appropriately, Bultmann's house, in Marburg, in Germany, proved to be on a hill, on Calvinstrasse. Mrs. Bultmann, a matronly lady dressed in gray, greeted me at the door, took my coat, and at once accompanied me into her husband's study.

"Will you have a pipe?" Bultmann said, taking a few steps toward me, which revealed a pronounced limp.

"Many thanks, I don't smoke," I replied.

Bultmann looked me up and down. He had a prudent eye, and the succinct, detached manner of someone who doesn't suffer fools gladly. He was dressed, rather carelessly, in a gray pin-striped suit and a very wide gray tie. After a few moments, he sat down by a round table that was almost a duplicate of Barth's. Mrs. Bultmann took a chair near him, and so did I.

"It's not a very nice day out," Bultmann said, in a voice that was thin and querulous. "I feel the changes of the weather in my head. It's not the wetness or the winter that I mind but the continual changes of the weather from day to day. But I am over eighty now."

I asked him whether he and Mrs. Bultmann had thought of living in a warmer, more stable climate.

"My husband loves this house," Mrs. Bultmann said. "He would not be happy anywhere else. He gets fresh air here. He walks out on the terrace."

"I can't walk very much now," Bultmann said. "From my childhood, I have had trouble with my left leg."

"My husband recently celebrated his eightieth birthday," Mrs. Bultmann said. "We told all our friends that we didn't want any celebration, but we had lots of telegrams and cards and long letters and short letters. The dean of the theology faculty of the University of Marburg, the rector of the university, and the Minister of Culture from Wiesbaden all came, and stayed for two hours. Two of our daughters made music for us. Our third daughter, who lectures on library science at Syracuse University, in America, arrived late and didn't have time to practice with her sisters."

"For my eightieth birthday my students gave me a third *Festschrift*," Bultmann said. "I've been spending all my time since then writing to each of the contributors."

To lead up to the subject of demythologizing, I asked Bultmann if he had any common ground with Barth.

"We both started out being opposed to liberal theology and its argument that men were religious by nature," he said. "Both Barth and I thought that this made religion too subjective. For us, God was an objective occurrence in the world. After that, we parted company. I don't read much Barth now. He's too orthodox—he believes in the literal word. I think philosophy and theology should be combined, but he doesn't. He doesn't like me, or Paul Tillich, for bringing in philosophy—he likes Brunner even less—but he and I still have very amusing exchanges." (Before coming to Marburg, I had spent a little time with Brunner in Zurich. Between playing Bach's Prelude in B Minor on the piano and playing Bach's Prelude in C Major, he had told me that though Barth and he were nearly of the same age—Brunner was almost seventy-six—and of the same nationality, lived only sixty miles apart, and had both started out as dialectical theologians, they had rarely met. Explaining that such conduct was by no means an oddity in the scholarly world, Brunner had gone on to quote a sort of theological justification that Barth had offered a B.B.C. interviewer who had asked about the chilly relationship existing between the two Swiss theologians: " 'In his good creation, God saw fit to create such diverse creatures as an elephant and a whale. Each has his own function and purpose. But they are so different that they cannot communicate with each other or even fight with each other. As a result, they also cannot conclude a peace pact with each other. Why God chose to place such diverse creatures in the same universe no one knows. For the answer to this question we must wait until the eschaton. Only then will it become clear as to why God created the elephant and the whale.' " In 1960, however, a common friend had managed to arrange a meeting between the whale and the elephant, and they had got on famously, posing with Mrs. Brunner and Mrs. Barth for several photographs.)

"Yes," Mrs. Bultmann said. "When Barth was bringing out the booklet 'Rudolf Bultmann—An Attempt to Understand Him,' he sent a copy of it to my husband with a letter opening 'O Angel, forgive me'—a line borrowed from the last scene of 'Figaro.' "

"What are the limits of demythologizing?" I asked. "I know that students of Barth have said it can be the death of religion if it is carried too far."

"There are no limits," Bultmann said. "I think we should take it as far as it can go."

"After the Second World War, I worked in a hospital in Marburg," Mrs. Bultmann put in. "Ministers used to preach to the wounded and disabled soldiers about sin, and so on, and it didn't mean anything to them. Professor Bultmann's and Professor Tillich's religion did mean something. Every Sunday, even now, I read aloud to Professor Bultmann a sermon of Tillich's."

"In any case, all I want to say about demythologizing I have said in my books," Bultmann said. "I now have only one task left. I must finish writing my commentary on the Epistles of John. After this task is finished, my work is done."

"Last year was the first time he missed going to the reunion of his pupils," Mrs. Bultmann said. "He wasn't well enough. But I came back and told him everything that had happened—the debates and the controversies." The reunion that Bultmann had missed for the first time was of his own "school"—all the people who had studied with him—which, I had discovered earlier by talking to a Bultmannian, numbered in the hundreds and met annually in a sort of academic convention. The coherence of the school could be judged by the fact that within that large school was a smaller school made up of the members of The Graeca, or "circle"—students who over the years had studied with Bultmann and had met with him once a week to read aloud classical literature over some wine.

Soon afterward, again in deference to an elderly man's health, I left Bultmann.

The late Dietrich Bonhoeffer has probably affected more Christian theologians and, through them, more Christians of every sort than any other one theologian of our time. Indeed, Bonhoeffer was at the center of the labyrinth disclosed by "Honest to God," all paths eventually leading to him. An observer has said of him, "Bonhoeffer has been sweeping through the theological world like a fire. You have only to look at the footnotes of the books on theology published in the last decade to know this is true." And, surprisingly, the fire was kindled by the small, fragmentary volume called "Letters and Papers from Prison," which was edited posthumously by Bonhoeffer's closest friend, Pastor Eberhard Bethge, who also arranged for its publication. The book is a collection of miscellaneous jottings, poems, miniature sermons, essays, and letters to his family and his friend Pastor Bethge, many of these being routine and only a few meditative—all written over a period of two years or so, beginning after he was arrested by the Nazis in April, 1943, as a suspected member of the Resistance and going up almost to the time of his death, in the concentration camp of Flossenburg, in April, 1945. Quite apart from the literary and chronological limitations that are inherent in any such collection, many of the printed letters dwell on the prisoner's daily needs, his regrets over his plight, and the wavering prospects for his release. Moreover, the editor has seen fit to omit a majority of the letters for family and other reasons, and Bonhoeffer, even though his letters were smuggled out, could not be unmindful of the prison censors. The result is that one shares Bonhoeffer's uneasy feeling that he is writing with someone reading over his shoulder. But at other times, because the letters were intended to be private, the reader feels a different embarrassment—as though he himself were an intruder. In addition, such theological reflections as Bonhoeffer was able to set down (they take up no more than fifty pages) bear the marks of intellectual isolation and of the abnormal conditions in Nazi Germany during the Second World War—circumstances that have to be taken into account in evaluating Bonhoeffer's ideas. Finally, the theological letters, instead of presenting his own views, record, as a rule, his objections to certain theologies and established religious practices, so there are only tantalizing hints of his constructive thinking. It is nothing less than extraordinary, then, that his book, with so many limitations, should have influenced a whole generation of theologians. The books of Robinson and van Buren, among others, would, by their authors' own testimony, have been inconceivable without the "Letters and Papers from Prison." Edwards, the publisher of "Honest to God," sees an even closer connection between Bonhoeffer and his successors. During my conversation with him, he compared Robinson and Bonhoeffer: "The life Robinson led was very much like that of Bonhoeffer. Both had to come to terms with secularism, one in the Resistance, one in Southwark. Bonhoeffer, like John Robinson, came from a very well-connected background. He saw nothing but intellectuals and Christians till he decided to join the Resistance. Again, like Robinson's experience with the South-wark parishioners, Bonhoeffer found that many non-believing soldiers and conspirators he was with had better values than the Christians with whom he had been brought up." However pervasive Bonhoeffer's influence, he has nevertheless had his critics, particularly among the theological elders, like Tillich, who said, "Everyone is always quoting 'Letters and Papers from Prison.' Bonhoeffer's martyrdom has given him authority—martyrdom always gives psychological authority—but in fact he didn't live long enough for us to know what he thought." Bonhoeffer was thirty-nine when he died.

To penetrate the aura of martyrdom, I decided to seek out one or two of the men who had known Bonhoeffer. Two who had known him well, it appeared, were Pastor Bethge, who had met him in 1935, and another pastor, Wolf-Dieter Zimmer-mann, who had met him a few years earlier, and had recently brought out "Begegnungen mit Dietrich Bonhoeffer—Ein Al-manach," a collection of reminiscences about the theologian by members of his family and by friends who had known him since childhood. I met Pastor Zimmermann first—in his two-story house, on Wichernstrasse, in a good residential area of West Berlin. Pastor Zimmermann, a rather smooth-looking man in gray flannels, who spoke English with a sprinkling of Americanisms, made both of us comfortable in very modern chairs in his living room, and had time to tell me only that he was a religious editor for radio and television, with a two-hour radio slot to fill each week, before a lady in a red-and-blue plaid skirt and a blue sweater entered with a sprightly step, carrying a tea tray on which were not only a teapot and its accessories but a bowl of soup. This was Mrs. Zimmermann. I stood up as she entered. She put down the tray, touched me on the arm, and said, "We German women aren't used to men standing up," and left.

"If you don't mind, I'll eat my dinner now," Pastor Zimmermann said, taking some pills with the soup. "Some people smoke: I have to take pills."

I had found Zimmermann's collection of reminiscences somewhat opaque, and now I asked him if he, as an editor, was satisfied with the picture of Bonhoeffer that emerged from it.

"When I came to collect the material for that book, I discovered that it was very difficult to get information about Bonhoeffer," Pastor Zimmermann said. "Several professors whom I asked to write about him replied that they remembered him only vaguely. The three groups who did remember him, and contributed to the collection, were his family, his pupils, and his personal friends. But his pupils never numbered more than a hundred and fifty all told, and only half of them were what one might call close to him, and half of *these* died in the war. His personal friends all remembered certain observations he made, or little things about him, that didn't suffice to make a picture. Strangely, I myself can remember him dressed only in light colors, though I know he must have had at least one dark suit for church purposes."

I asked him how he had first met Bonhoeffer.

"Well, it was in 1932, when I began attending his lectures on the Nature of the Church, at the University of Berlin," he said. "I remember that his lectures were very theoretical. At that time, he was a *Privatdozent* in Theology, and, with his kind of career behind him, it was clear that if things went along normally, he would soon be a professor. He told me he would like all of us, his students, to meet with him once a week and discuss some of the theoretical problems he was lecturing on. At the time, he was living in his parents' house in Grunewald—a prosperous and rather exclusive area, where many professors lived—and Bonhoeffer didn't want us to meet there. He didn't want to have a boss-and-student relationship, he wanted a more normal relationship, and he asked me if the group might meet in my room.

I was living near the Alexanderplatz, a working-class neighborhood, and we met there. That was the situation in which I knew him, and I find that my life has been interpenetrated by his."

"What were your impressions of him at the time?" I asked.

"I don't remember him as a terribly good theologian, in the sense that he was good at theory," Pastor Zimmermann said. "Yet, as theologians, go, he was a more normal person than most. He was a bit arrogant, a bit intellectual, a bit isolated and lonely, a bit narcissistic. He was the narcissistic type. He looked in his own mirror."

I asked the Pastor what he meant by that, and instead of replying he said, "You see, he did everything early. He received the Licentiate of Theology when he was twenty-one. He was quick at picking up things. He had never done any high jumping, for instance, but when, in his student days, they had a competition for high jumping at the university, he simply went out on the field and jumped higher than anyone else. He was able to do many things this way. He loved playing tennis, and he was very good at table tennis, too. He played the piano, sometimes in the morning and then after lunch and then after dinner and then at two o'clock in the morning. As a child, he went about learning things as a grownup would. He had discipline. He would set an hour a day aside to go and play tennis, say, and then he would come back and read and reread books. He read all the time. One day, Bonhoeffer and I and a friend of mine were camping in the woods two hours north of here— I say a friend of *mine* because Bonhoeffer never really made friends. Well, he did make friends with Pastor Bethge, but Bethge, a very quiet, shy man, was a good sounding board for Bonhoeffer. Anyway, the three of us were sitting on a little hill by a brook at sunset, and my friend said to Bonhoeffer, who was reading a book on Christology, 'Bonhoeffer, look, there is such a lovely sunset.' Bonhoeffer look up for barely a second. A thrilled expression came over his face, but he immediately went back to reading. That was typical of him. He had seen the sunset and had been thrilled by it, and now could go back to Christology."

I asked what he thought was the extent of Bonhoeffer's influence in Germany now.

"As it happens, in West Germany today his influence is fragmentary," Pastor Zimmermann said. "There are a lot of youth hostels named 'Bonhoeffer,' and the German Evangelical Church accepts certain elements of his theology, but no one in West Germany accepts him completely. Curiously, his influence is considerable in the Communist countries. In East Germany, the C.D.U.—the Christian Democratic Union—has taken Bonhoeffer over. So has the Prague Peace Movement. They find Bonhoeffer's religionless Christianity perfect for them."

I had to catch my breath. I had come across some pat speculation in newspapers that Communism, as it finally moved into the twentieth century, was discarding some of its nineteenth-century luggage, like the dogma of scientific materialism, just as capitalism had abandoned some of its inherited doctrines, such as rugged individualism; in different ways, it was thought, both were putting aside antiquated ideologies, and from opposite sides both were developing the same sort of welfare state. It was, in fact, argued that in this convergence lay the hope for a reunified Germany, which might one day become a bridge between the East and the West. Even in the context of such speculation, however, the adoption of a Christian martyr by a Communist country seemed bizarre, and now I said as much to Pastor Zimmermann.

"You know, in our scholarly tradition in Germany we divide theoretical thinking from practical action," he said. "This goes so far that a professor isn't supposed to do anything practical. I mean, things have changed a bit since the war, but before that we used to have people who would just sit somewhere and think. Kant was such a thinker—you know, he spent all his time sitting and thinking in Königsberg, that one little town. He never left the town—wrote all his books there. Similarly, for centuries after the Reformation the churches of the German states were separated from real life. They were governed by the states. In all that time, the only alternative to the state ethics was pietism. In 1919, when the Kirchenbund, a very loose federation of the independent provincial churches, established in 1871, finally got a little authority, and there could be such a thing as a church social ethic that was different from the social ethic of the state, this independence created a lot of problems, because the Church had had no experience in ruling itself. Bonhoeffer's book 'Act and Being' was concerned with this problem: What is a Christian ethic in everyday life? This problem became all the more important when the Church capitulated to the state once again, under Nazism, at which time the dream of the National Church was finally realized. The German Evangelical Church was established only in 1945, but it still does not enjoy much authority, as the provincial churches go on maintaining quite a lot of their independence."

Pastor Zimmermann concluded, "You know, Bonhoeffer told me dozens of time, beginning as early as 1933, that he wanted to die at the age of thirty-nine. He did die at the age of thirty-nine. When I asked him why he wanted to die early, he said that life should be going up and up and up, that he didn't want to grow old, lose some of his powers, become senile, lose some of his intelligence, lose a certain physical facility. He didn't want to go down."

Bonhoeffer had been dead just twenty years. He had left behind him a fairly substantial record, in the letters and papers he wrote, and in such of his books as "Sanctorum Communio," "Act and Being," "Life Together," and "The Cost of Discipleship," yet the outline of his life had already begun to lose sharp definition. (Even the translations of his books fail to do him justice. The English one of "Letters and Papers" abounds in errors, such as "piano" for *"Klavichord,"* and "sensitive gums" for *"empfindlichen Gaumen."*) Pastor Zimmermann, for example, considered Bonhoeffer to have predicted his death at the age of thirty-nine, whereas a number of theologians I had talked with who had also known Bonhoeffer gave different versions, one saying that Bonhoeffer had always hoped to live to be fifty, another declaring he had never given a thought to death, and Roger Manvell and Heinrich Fraenkel, in their book "The Men Who Tried to Kill Hitler," wrote, "Even as early as 1933 he [Bonhoeffer] had told his friend Pastor Zimmermann that he wanted, after a full life, to die young at the age of thirty-eight. This was his age when the Nazis assassinated him in 1945." It brought one up short, especially since Terence Prittie, in another book on the Resistance, "Germans Against Hitler," had also written that Bonhoeffer "was under thirty-eight when he was murdered." Actually, both discrepancies could best be explained as printing errors, since all the accounts recorded Bonhoeffer's dates accurately as February, 1906, to April, 1945. And, in any event, if Bonhoeffer had expected to die at an early age, why should the "Letters and Papers," chronicling his last two years, have centered, as they did, on aspirations for the future? Some letters showed him considering the coming years with hope, as he awaited the emergence of a better Germany. Some revealed his thoughts on what the role of the Church should be in a defeated Germany. Other papers were in fact notes or outlines for books he expected to write one day.

Even allowing for the fact that a martyr by the manner of his death brings idolaters to life (and in the past it has sometimes taken centuries to see through to the martyr as he was), it was still jarring to come up against such conflicts of testimony. Then I recalled one of Bonhoeffer's letters, written a few months before his death: "I remember talking to a young French pastor at A. thirteen years ago. We were discussing what our real purpose was in life. He said he would like to become a saint. I think it is quite likely he did become one. At the time I was very much impressed, though I disagreed with him, and said I should prefer to have faith, or words to that effect." The portentousness of the remark—and, one could almost say, the prescience of it—unsettled me further. I felt I was just beginning to see the deeper meaning of the ungainly word "demythologize." I began to wonder if, without quite being aware of it, I might not have been put in touch with the authentic Bonhoeffer by something that Paul Lehmann, a professor of theology at Union Theological Seminary, had once told me. He had been Bonhoeffer's best American friend—he insisted that Bonhoeffer had a great capacity for friendship—and he had seen him for the last time on Bonhoeffer's second, and last, visit to America, in 1939. Lehmann had said to me, "Dietrich had come from a country where only the best was encouraged, only the best could get on. This was very evident in him. He once said to me that somebody who was as bad at tennis as I was had no business occupying the court. This was characteristic of him, and very Germanic. He was very good at tennis." But then Lehmann, too, had turned reverent: "You see, Dietrich was rather like a Greek god. His blond hair was the only physical thing that told you he was German. He had perfect proportions; he was a very handsome man. In 1949, I met Pastor Bethge for the first time. I took to him in exactly the same way I had taken to Bonhoeffer. It was as though Pastor Bethge and I had known each other from the very start, and, in a sense, we had, for we were both close friends of Dietrich's. Our immediately taking to one another like that was the kind of spiritual community that Bonhoeffer had written about in 'Sanctorum Communio.'"

It was Pastor Bethge who, through the "Letters and Papers," was responsible for first bringing Bonhoeffer to public notice, and he had since established himself as the principal authority on Bonhoeffer. He was married to one of Bonhoeffer's nieces, and had access to all the family letters and papers. From 1945 on, he had devoted himself to studying the life and work of his friend, and now he was engaged in collecting and editing his papers, and in writing his biography. Bonhoeffer, over the last ten years of his life, when he was struggling toward his fateful decision to commit himself to the Resistance, made Bethge his confidant, and over his last two years, when, as a prisoner, he was denied a "father confessor," gratefully allowed Bethge, through correspondence, to take on that office as well. (Though the identity of the recipient of some of the most important letters in "Letters and Papers" was originally withheld, it was revealed, as soon as the book became well known, that they were addressed to the editor himself.)

Recently, when, after immersing myself in Bonhoeffer literature, I spent some time with Pastor Bethge in Germany and, in the hope of unwinding the tangled skein of Bonhoeffer's life, I asked Pastor Bethge to "interpret" Bonhoeffer (in the special Bultmannian sense, as it were) for me and explain the contradictions in the theologian's life, Pastor Bethge told me that Bonhoeffer's life could be understood in terms of the Bonhoeffer family. The traits of his character, his decision to take up the study of theology, even his martyrdom—all had their sources in the family, in some cases as far back as four generations. (Most of the Bonhoeffer family was involved in the Resistance, and a brother and two brothers-in-law were imprisoned with Dietrich.)

His father, Karl Bonhoeffer, was descended from a Dutch clan that settled in Württemberg, Germany, in 1513. Originally goldsmiths, in time they had become a leading family of lawyers, ministers, and doctors in the Freie Reichsstad. The family seal shows a lion with a bundle of beans in his paw on a blue ground, the word "Bonhoeffer" meaning "beanfield." Karl had grown up in Swabia, a predominantly agricultural or forested region that contains the Black Forest, and is associated with the names of such literary and philosophical figures as Schelling, Schiller, Hegel, and now Bultmann. As a child, Karl was regularly required by his father to walk forty kilometres from the family home, in Tübingen, to Stuttgart, where his grandmother lived. Karl's father was himself so fond of walking that, for short journeys, he thought trains too slow; it was said that in the spring he would go for walks in the Schwäbische Alb carrying bags of radish seeds that he would sow along the way, returning in autumn for the harvest. Karl took after his father, and, as a man, used to go for long walks, gathering mushrooms. Sometimes he would take Dietrich with him, and instruct his son in how to distinguish the edible varieties from the poisonous ones. The mushrooms would be brought home, dried, and served at the table. Dietrich grew up to be a great walker and a mushroom collector. Karl, after an exacting university career, had become a well-known physician, an authority on neurology and psychiatry. (There was an indirect mention of him in Ernest Jones' biography of Freud.) Because of the background of the father, the Bonhoeffer household was solidly grounded in science. Karl's working day was fairly leisurely. He would go to the local clinic, in Breslau, where he had made his home and where the family lived until Dietrich was six, at nine-thirty and return home at two. He might see two or three patients in the afternoon, but that was all. Like an Englishman, he always had the air, however busy he might be, of someone with unlimited time at his disposal. He was a man of few words, however, and always talked to the point. If the children spoke up too vociferously at the dinner table, Karl brushed their remarks aside with a few well-chosen words that left them in no doubt that what they had said was nonsense. Later on, his letters to imprisoned members of his family were simple and controlled. He was incapable of grandiose words or grandiose sentiments.

Dietrich's mother was the former Paula von Hase, the daughter of Klara von Hase, née Countess Kalckreuth. Paula's father had been a chaplain to the Emperor, and her grandfather a nineteenth-century church historian of some distinction. She had blond hair and blue eyes, whereas her husband had black hair and brown eyes, and she was a contrast to him in practically every other way as well. Dietrich's looks, his feeling for music, and his exuberant spirits are said to have come from her. She had a keen interest in other people and a way of coming up with quick solutions to their problems. She was spirited, and she had an engaging manner. She was, as a rule, controlled, and when, during the First World War, Walter, her second son, who was a patriot and something of a poet, was dying in France of wounds received in battle, her sense of duty to Germany restrained her from rushing to his bedside, as her instincts prompted her to do. After Walter's death, however, she bitterly regretted this restraint, for she felt she might have nursed her son back to health, and as a consequence she was ill for half a year. It was the family custom to write down the significant events in the life of the family at the end of each year, but for ten years after Walter's death there were no entries. During the Second World War, when two of her other sons, Dietrich and Klaus, and also her two sons-in-law, Hans von Dohnanyi and Rüdiger Schleicher, had been imprisoned under suspicion of plotting against Hitler, she thrust herself upon the City Commandant of Berlin, Paul von Hase, who was her cousin, and, demanding that he intervene, succeeded in having the conditions of their imprisonment made less rigorous. All during their imprisonment, she poured her heart out to them in high-flown letters, but after they died, she tried hard not to give way as she had after Walter died. She had always been musical (Saturday evenings in the Bonhoeffer household were set aside for music) and had a special weakness for Schumann lieder. She had often sung, with Dietrich accompanying her on the piano. Later, when he was in Finkenwalde Seminary, he kept up the family tradition by organizing a quintet, of which he was the pianist. No matter how inadequate the other players were, it is said, he was able to lead them into giving a respectable performance.

Dietrich grew up in Berlin, to which the family moved from Breslau. In Berlin, the Bonhoeffers lived on Wangenheimstrasse, in the Grunewald district, in a large house appointed with heavy oak furniture and heavy velvet draperies. The walls were hung with paintings, among them pleasant landscapes by Dietrich's great-grandfather Stanislaus Graf Kalckreuth and portraits by his great-uncle Leopold Graf Kalckreuth, of which some hang today in an art gallery in Hamburg. There were five servants, including a governess, who spoke French with the children, and a personal maid for Mrs. Bonhoeffer. The district, like the house, was upper bourgeois, with an academic flavor (Harnack and Max Planck lived there), and the Bonhoeffers themselves were members of the cultivated upper middle class. Altogether, there were eight Bonhoeffer children—Karl Friedrich, Walter, Klaus, Ursula, Christine, Dietrich and his twin sister, Sabine, and Suzanne, in that order. Every one of Dietrich's brothers and sisters had an important place in his life.

Karl Friedrich grew up to be a biochemist. He had studied with Max Planck and was on friendly terms with Einstein. He undertook research on heavy water, but in the thirties he left it for the study of the interaction between leaves and the air. Karl Friedrich had been in the First World War, with Walter, and because of that he enjoyed a certain prestige in the Bonhoeffer household. It was due to his influence that Dietrich, to assert himself and have a domain of his own, first turned to theology—something out of favor among the Bonhoeffers, and even ridiculed. The Bonhoeffers were not a churchgoing family, and all the family baptisms, weddings, and funerals were performed in the house by an uncle, who was a pastor, and, even so, was the victim of a certain amount of derision, as was another uncle, whose interest in the family genealogy had led him to claim that the Bonhoeffers were descendants—very remote ones—of Luther.

Walter, who aspired to be a biologist or a zoologist, modelled his poems after Hölderlin, who, in his turn, had been influenced by Schiller. Walter was a bit of a stoic. The hours before his death found him composing a letter about how he had anesthetized the pain of his wounds by thinking about his comrades-in-arms. Owing to his influence, Dietrich was a nationalist in the twenties, though in the thirties his detestation of Nazism made him turn pacifist for a time.

Klaus was the adventurer in the family. He was fond of travelling, and had once gone to Spain, where he became an enthusiast of bullfighting, bought a painting by the then unknown Picasso (or he later came to think that it was by Picasso), and enjoyed the society of aristocrats; in fact, he made a hobby of studying the aristocracies of other countries. Klaus was responsible, along with Ursula and Christine and their husbands, for Dietrich's becoming involved in the Resistance. Christine, the cleverest of the Bonhoeffer girls, as the wife of Hans von Dohnanyi (Hans' father, Ernst, was the well-known pianist and composer, and Hans' son, Christoph, is now a conductor of the West German Radio Orchestra in Cologne), was the Bonhoeffer woman closest to the plot, and it was her great sorrow that she had not been born a man.

Next in line were the twins, Dietrich and Sabine, he taking after their mother in appearance, she after their father. Sabine, too, had her part in the conspiracy of the family. She had married a Jew—Gerhard Leibholz, the youngest professor of political economy in Berlin (he is now a judge of the West German Supreme Court)—and when the Bonhoeffers learned that Hitler was about to decree that all Jews must have their passports stamped "J" (for men) or "S" (for women), they got

Sabine and her husband across the French border, from which they made their way to England. Not only did the Leibholzes, who passed the war in Oxford, dramatize the Jewish predicament for Dietrich but Gerhard Leibholz wrote speeches for George K. A. Bell, the Bishop of Chichester, who became a British spokesman for the plotters.

Suzanne, who married a church historian named Walter Dress, also played a role in the plot, but a very minor one—she infrequently smuggled messages to and from her imprisoned brothers. During the war, she was busy with the bringing up of two small children.

In the eyes of the Bonhoeffer parents, Dietrich was neither the cleverest of their children (Karl Friedrich was regarded as that) nor the most daring or heroic (Walter had died at the front). In fact, after the war they found it very interesting that Dietrich, because of Bethge, should have become the best-known member of the family. Even as children, the dominant figures in the household had been the three elder brothers, in contrast to whom Dietrich was classed with Sabine and Suzanne as one of "the little ones." The elder brothers were all aggressively agnostic and intellectual, and were all interested in science. They contributed to the secular atmosphere of the household, and at Christmas, more often than not, the boys' presents were books on science. From the very beginning, Dietrich exchanged his books for Suzanne's, which were likely to be more reflective and literary.

Although Dr. and Mrs. Bonhoeffer were not inclined to force their children in any direction, they did once present Dietrich to Leonid Kreutzer, the distinguished pianist, then a professor at the State Academy of Music, in Berlin, to find out how gifted the boy was in music and whether he should think about becoming a pianist. Dietrich, however, took his future into his own hands. As a matter of course, all boys studied Latin, Greek, and French in the *Gymnasium,* and in the last two years of school they added a fourth language, of their choice, which was most often English, but Dietrich returned from school one day and informed his mother that as his fourth language he had chosen Hebrew. The decision meant only one thing—that Dietrich was going to be a theologian—and he had reached it all alone. An average student, he made his *Abitur* in 1923 and proceeded to the University of Tübingen, as his brothers had before him. He studied there for a year, attending lectures in theology, as well as in philosophy and epistemology. After a summer in Italy and North Africa, he moved to the University of Berlin, where he studied first with the aging Harnack, and then, in turn, with Karl Holl and Reinhold Seeberg, both of them leaders of the Lutheran renaissance. He received the Licentiate of Theology in 1927, at the age of twenty-one, having studied for it under Seeberg's direction. Bonhoeffer had settled on Seeberg because Seeberg seemed to him the weakest professor and therefore the one who would allow him the greatest independence. Bonhoeffer's thesis, entitled "Sanctorum Communio: A Dogmatic Investigation of the Sociology of the Church" and written, oddly, in the incompatible traditions of Barth and Troeltsch, was concerned with the Church in its dual role as a heavenly institution and an earthly power. (Barth, who during the lifetime of Bonhoeffer was cool to his work, called this dissertation in 1955 "far more instructive and stimulating and illuminating and genuinely edifying reading today than many of the more famous works which have since been written on the problem of the church.") In 1927, Bonhoeffer took the first of two theological examinations that were required of anyone wishing to become a pastor, and went as a curate to Barcelona, which had a German colony estimated at six thousand. The Protestant congregation, however, numbered no more than three hundred, of whom fewer than fifty were regular churchgoers. There he read the writings of the late Albert Schweitzer and began questioning the kind of future that Christianity could have in Europe. He also read a good deal about Buddhism in an effort to discover in that religion an alternative to the Christian solution to the problem of power and, more specifically, to the Lutheran solution to the problem: that the exercise of power was sinful but men had to exercise it in the name of responsibility. His wish to find an alternative to the Christian solution rose out of his dissatisfaction with the hierarchy of the established church and its system of privileges, though at the time he took it for granted that organized religion was necessary. He apparently made a great impression on the children in his congregation by telling them Bible stories as though they might be fairy tales.

After a year in Spain, Bonhoeffer returned to Berlin, where he worked on and finished his *Habilitationsschrift*—a dissertation required for admission to a theological faculty in Germany. Published as "Act and Being: Transcendental Philosophy and Ontology in Systematic Theology," it dealt with the problem of God's continuity and contingency in the world, and ended what Bethge came to regard as the first of Bonhoeffer's three theological phases. This phase, which began with "Sanctorum Communio," was a mixture of Barth's "Word of God," or "revelation," theology—dominant in the twenties—with Troeltsch's sociological approach. Of Bonhoeffer's thought in this period Bethge has written, "We usually think of concreteness in terms of the application after the explanation of the text. But this separation into two additional activities in order to grasp the revelation is precisely what Bonhoeffer was fighting. . . . Concreteness is to be understood not as an addition or second activity but as a genuine attribute of revelation itself. . . . There is no God, Bonhoeffer emphasizes, other than the incarnated one known to us and meeting and claiming us in the 'Christ existing as the community of men,' the Church."

The middle period was a sort of bridge between the relatively peaceful existence of an academic theologian and the perilous life of a conspirator. It was a restive period, in which an intellectual was transformed into a practical churchman, and in which Bonhoeffer was forced by circumstances to take positions that in retrospect seemed to have made his role in the Resistance inevitable. In 1930, Bonhoeffer was awarded a fellowship to Union Theological Seminary in New York, and came to the United States for a year. He was not excited by the American theologians he encountered. On the contrary, he found them inadequately informed about the theology of revelation, and, though he himself was now moving away from it, he started defending it, in order to introduce American theologians to Barth. He found nearly all the sermons in America vacuous, probably because sermons in Germany, though dull, always had intellectual substance, and the American tradition of inspirational preaching was wholly unfamiliar to him. He made friends with Lehmann and also with the pacifist Jean Lasserre. (With Lasserre he drove to Mexico during the summer holidays.) He was drawn to Negro churches, and spent Sundays in Harlem, where he acquired a taste for Negro spirituals. At the end of his year in America, he thought of going home by way of India, in order to deepen his understanding, this time, of Gandhiism and Hinduism, but he did not want to go alone and could not find anyone to make the journey with him, so he went home the way he had come, except that he spent some time in Bonn with Barth, and attended a World Alliance Conference in Cambridge, before settling down in Berlin. There, after ordination, he taught courses in Systematic Theology at the University of Berlin, served as a student-chaplain—preaching regularly—at the Technical Academy in Berlin-Charlottenburg, conducted a confirmation class in Wedding, founded a settlement house there, and became a secretary of the Youth Commission of the World Alliance for International Friendship Through the Churches and of the Universal Christian Council for Life and Work. He was a *Privatdozent* at the University of Berlin (a step toward an eventual professorship), and was still living in the genteel bourgeois ambience he had known as a boy, but he was gradually beginning to be caught up in practical work for the Church. In Berlin, as in Barcelona, he made an impression on the children. He read opera librettos with his confirmation candidates, and took them to hear performances. Most of the boys died at the front or in concentration camps, but a number of letters they wrote to Bonhoeffer survive and testify that his influence on them lasted as long as they lived.

What was now happening in Germany was so momentous that no one could stand aloof, least of all a Christian interested in pastoral work. In July, 1933, church elections were held all over Germany, and as a result of Hitler's intervention Nazis took over more than seventy per cent of the positions on the ecclesiastical governing bodies—a prelude to the "Brown Synod," so named because the majority of the delegates attended wearing the brown shirts of the S.A. This General Synod of the Prussian Provincial Church (Preussische Landeskirche), which was by far the largest provincial church, was assembled that September in Berlin, and it introduced into the Church constitution the Aryan clause, already operative in the state. Since there were only something like twenty pastors with Jewish blood out of a total of twenty thousand, and since they alone were affected, most pastors, taking the view that the action of the Brown Synod made little actual difference, were prepared to prove their Aryan heritage. Bonhoeffer was so deeply disappointed by the reactions of his superiors in the university and in the Church that he decided to leave them both and become pastor of two small, independent German-speaking congregations in London. Over the protests of his colleagues, but with the encouragement of his parents, who wanted him out of Nazi Germany, he broke with his country and his past, choosing the simple life of a pastor and practical involvement in the Church in preference to the comfortable academic career for which his family background and his years of study had prepared him. He went to England in October, 1933, accompanied by a pastor named Franz Hildebrandt, who is half Jewish. Hildebrandt, at that time Bonhoeffer's best friend, had to leave Germany, because of his Jewish blood. Pastor Hildebrandt took up in London some of the clerical duties of Bonhoeffer, who, in turn, shared with him both his house and his salary.

In England, Bonhoeffer formed a friendship with George Bell, the Bishop of Chichester, and he also met C. F. Andrews, the biographer of Gandhi, and Marilyn Slade, the Englishwoman who had taken the Indian name Mirabhi and had become a follower of Gandhi. The influence of Andrews and Mirabhi led Bonhoeffer to toy once more with the idea of going to India, particularly since he now thought that Gandhi's ideas about nonviolence might be used to resist Hitler in Germany. In the meantime, in Germany, the Brown Synod had provoked the beginnings of organized resistance within the Church by a group originally two thousand strong called the Pastors' Emergency League, which by the end of that year had tripled its clerical strength. Then, in May and October, 1934, this group had convened synods of its own, in Barmen and Dahlen, which solemnly declared the Deutsche Christen, or Nazi church government, to be heretical, and set up an emergency church government—the Brethren Councils of the Confessing Church. (In subsequent years, as Hitler consolidated his hold on Germany, the group all but disappeared.) In April, 1935, Bonhoeffer accepted a call from the Confessing Church to come back to Germany and head a seminary, and he became the guiding spirit of a small, newly founded seminary for Confessing Church ordinants in Finkenwalde, in Pomerania. It was here that he first met Pastor Bethge.

In Finkenwalde, Bonhoeffer established a community within a community—the Bruderhaus, or Brethren House, a sort of island of withdrawal from the world, which later became quite well known through his little book "Life Together." The tradition of monastic life was not associated with Protestantism. Indeed, ever since Luther's day any kind of monastic order was assumed by Germans to be Roman. Yet Bonhoeffer now tried to revive monastic life in Finkenwalde. While the members of the order did not take vows of poverty, chastity, and obedience, and were free to marry and leave the community at any time, they did try to live simply and own everything in common, the day being planned around prayer, the singing of hymns, and other devotional exercises. The inspiration for this life evidently emanated almost completely from Bonhoeffer himself. Pastor Bethge remembers that Bonhoeffer introduced a period of meditation as part of the daily routine, and that when he went away for a time the period of meditation was quickly abandoned. On his return, the members confessed to him that they didn't know what to meditate about. He instructed them: "Run after your thoughts, get them back, concentrate." But the natural exuberance of Bonhoeffer would often break up the routine that he himself had brought into existence. Sometimes for days it would be replaced by hiking or tennis or practicing chamber music together. In the evenings, the members might play bridge or quiz games. Characteristically, Bonhoeffer never laid down any rules. He made up procedures as he went along and revised them as practice required. Intellectual matters were not stressed, and he led the community in prayer in a childlike way that its members found touching. As part of the loose-knit routine, he introduced the custom of confession, and he made Pastor Bethge his confessor. He confided to Pastor Bethge that he distrusted theory in theology, that religion sometimes seemed to him "a big lie," that he felt himself guilty of doubt, pride, ambition, and intellectual arrogance. And a book he wrote during this period, "The Cost of Discipleship," which offers perhaps the best and most coherent statement of his views, shows him to be turning more and more to the person of Christ as the paradigm for all men—mapping out, in the words of Karl Barth, "a program in which we try to shape our lives by the example of the life of Jesus as sketched in the Gospels and the commandments which He gave to His own people and to all men generally." In Barth's estimation, the book was easily the best one ever written on the subject. About the first and the more original part of the book, he added, again in a post-humous salute in 1955, "The matter is handled with such depth and precision that I am almost tempted simply to reproduce them [the opening sections] in an extended quotation. For I cannot hope to say anything better on the subject than what is said here by a man who, having written on discipleship, was ready to achieve it in his own life, and did in his own way achieve it even to the point of death."

In 1937, the Nazis launched a campaign against the Confessing Church. They arrested hundreds of its pastors, sought to limit the effectiveness of others by forbidding them to travel, and, in September, dissolved Finkenwalde by force, though they let Bonhoeffer go free. The two years that followed were uncertain and confused for Bonhoeffer, but they were the gestation period of what was probably the most important decision of his life—to become a political conspirator against Hitler in the name of Christianity. As it happened, most of the people who took a leading part in the plot were Christians and intellectuals. Manvell and Fraenkel explained, "In its various forms, the heart of the German Resistance drew its strength from the Christian faith. . . . Though many thousands of men and women shared in the resistance movement as a whole, those who finally took action as principals in July, 1944, found the courage and resources to do so because of the reserves of the human spirit on which they knew they could draw in the event of catastrophe, torture, and violent death." Yet in Bonhoeffer's case the decision was apparently taken more on the basis of accidental and personal factors than as a result of careful deliberation either on the consequences of his participation or on any justification for it to be found in Christian doctrine. In 1940 he met Colonel Hans Oster, second in command of the *Abwehr,* or Military Intelligence Department. The *Abwehr* was headed by Admiral Wilhelm Canaris, who, though he was considered one of Hitler's right-hand men, was willing to avert his eyes from some of the treasonous activities that were going on in his department. Later, Oster was to take Bonhoeffer on as a secret agent and so put him beyond the reach of the Gestapo, and give him the opportunity—denied to all Germans, let alone the persecuted pastors of the Confessing Church—to travel in Europe and evade military service.

In March, 1939, Bonhoeffer went to London to visit his former congregations, and he also called on Reinhold Niebuhr, who happened to be teaching in Scotland at the time, and asked for help in getting to America for a year. Niebuhr immediately made plans for Bonhoeffer to teach at Union Theological Seminary that summer, and wrote to Lehmann about ways of arranging a longer stay for Bonhoeffer: "My concern is in regard to Bonhoeffer. He . . . is anxious to come to America to evade for the time being a call to the colors. . . . I am wondering whether you would be willing to constitute a committee with me, call me the chairman and yourself the secretary, and send out a mimeographed letter offering Bonhoeffer's services to colleges and universities. . . . You could have him give you topics and a description of his activities in behalf of the confessional synod. . . . Don't write him too much, but if you are willing to do this just tell him that you will get in touch with him as soon as he arrives at Union to work out plans which I have suggested. There will be some difficulty in getting him out, and if he fails he will land in prison. He has done a great work for the Church."

Lehmann could not have been more coöperative, and the suggested mimeographed letter was sent out in June, 1939, over his signature. It was an excellent introduction to Bonhoeffer at that time:

A committee, of which Dr. Reinhold Niebuhr, Professor of Applied Christianity at the Union Theological Seminary, New York, is the chairman, is venturing to bring to your attention the Reverend Dietrich Bonhoeffer, Licentiate in Theology. Reverend Mr. Bonhoeffer is one of the ablest of the younger theologians and one of the most courageous of the younger pastors who have undertaken the task of the faithful exposition and perpetuation of the Christian faith in the present critical time in Germany. He comes from a distinguished line of forebears both in the pulpit and in the university. . . . Among the more notable of Mr. Bonhoeffer's contributions to theological learning are three brilliant and profound volumes on "The Communion of Saints," "Act and Being," and one published only recently under the title "Life Together." During the academic year, 1930–1931, Mr. Bonhoeffer was a fellow in theology at Union Theological Seminary and after his return to Germany he began a promising theological career as *Privatdozent* in the theological faculty at Berlin. Political circumstances have interrupted these hopes. After a pastorate in the German Church in London, Mr. Bonhoeffer returned to his country and assumed the difficult responsibility of teaching the future ministers of the Confessional Church. Some time ago, his little seminary was closed by the government and he has been continuing his work since then in a private capacity in the parsonages of Pomerania. . . . If your institution has a lecture foundation or lecture series on a variety of problems, will you give favorable consideration to an invitation to Mr. Bonhoeffer to appear? He is in full command of the English language and prepared to discuss in a reliable and challenging manner problems of theology, philosophy, and the contemporary situation of Christianity in Germany. The committee is venturing to suggest an honorarium of not less than twenty-five dollars and, wherever possible, of fifty dollars. I hope very urgently that we may have some word from you at the earliest possible moment. . . . Your active cooperation in this venture will be a real expression of the spirit of ecumenical Christianity.

In the meantime, Bonhoeffer had reached America and had already begun to agonize over whether he should have come at all. He had thought that in the United States he would be able to make friends for the beleaguered Confessing Church as well as to find sanctuary from German military service, but one of the jobs that were found for him in America involved work with German refugees, and he was tormented with the fear that his association with these exiles would bar his return to Germany. He wrote to one of his American benefactors:

Before I left Germany, I had long talks with my brethren from the Brethren Council and pledged myself to return to Germany after about a year's time to take up the training work in the Confessing Church again. . . . From the point of view of the Confessing Church, my trip to America was meant to be an ecumenical link between our isolated Church in Germany and our friends over here. . . . All of us, of course, were well aware of the fact that it means running a risk for a Confessional pastor to go to America with the intention to go back to Germany, and we all agreed that I should take that risk and pay the price for it, if necessary, if it is of a true value to the Church of Christ there and here. But, of course, I must not for the sake of loyalty to the Confessing Church accept a post which on principle would make my return to Germany impossible. Now, my question is whether that would not be the case with any post that is officially concerned with refugee work? As a matter of fact, I am afraid, it would be so. Now, if that is true, what can we do about it? . . . Finally, let me add a very personal remark. My best friend in Germany, a young Confessional pastor, who has been working with me for many years [this was Pastor Bethge], will be in the same conflict with regard to military service, etc. at the latest by next spring, possibly in the fall of this year. I feel it would be an utmost disloyalty to leave him alone in Germany when the conflict comes up for him. I should either have to go back to stand by him and to act with him or to get him out and to share my living with him, whatever it be, though I do not know if he would be willing to leave Germany.

Bonhoeffer was on the verge of making his critical decision.

Only a week after his arrival in America, he decided to call
off his visit, cancel all the arrangements made for him, and
rush back to Germany while he was still able to do so. He
wrote that night in the Prophets Chamber at Union, "Quite
obviously, one was disappointed, even cross. For me it means
more than I can realize at present." And later he wrote to
Niebuhr, "I have had the time to think and to pray about my
situation and that of my nation and to have God's will for me
clarified. I have come to the conclusion that I have made a
mistake in coming to America. I must live through this difficult period of our national history with the Christian people of
Germany. I will have no right to participate in the reconstruction
of Christian life in Germany after the war if I do not share
the trials of this time with my people. . . . Christians in Germany
will face the terrible alternative of either willing the defeat of
their nation in order that Christian civilization may survive, or
willing the victory of their nation and thereby destroying our
civilization. I know which of these alternatives I must choose;
but I cannot make that choice in security."

The unease that Bonhoeffer felt throughout the American
episode was betrayed in his style, which was so repetitious and
overfull that not only did his touch sometimes appear lacking
in grace and tact but he left the impression that he himself
was not convinced by the reasons he gave for having come
to America in the first place and for then having abruptly
chosen to return. It happened that during Bonhoeffer's stay at
Union, Lehmann was teaching in Illinois, so that the two men
had to explain everything to each other by letters, and in inform-
ing Lehmann of his decision Bonhoeffer wrote:

Thank you so much for your good letter, which is so full of
friendship and hope for the future. I find it very hard to tell you
that I have decided in the meantime to return to Germany in a few
weeks. The invitation I got to come to America was based on the
misunderstanding that I would stay here for good. I was supposed

to supervise the social welfare of the Christian refugees, which meant that I could never go back to Germany. Now all necessary decisions have been made and I have informed the Church about it, and I shall return in July or August. I regret it for various reasons; on the other hand, I am very glad to give a helping hand over there. I am drawn toward my fighting brothers; I am sure you will understand me. And now I have a very urgent request to make: In your very kind letters to the colleges you mentioned my work in Pomerania. If such a letter gets into the hands of the German authorities, the whole of my job would be finished. Will you understand me if I ask you kindly and at the same time urgently, to write to the same people that I have returned in the meantime and the whole thing did not come off and perhaps also (which would be important to me) that this whole undertaking was based on a misunderstanding. I hope that they are reliable enough not to circulate the letters any further. . . . I am sorry for all the trouble I have given you. Please see to it that people just think that the whole matter is finished. And please do not mention in your letter Pomerania again, and also not that the matter should not get into the hands of the German authorities. Just say simply that "the matter regarding Mr. D. B. was in the meantime settled as he has returned to Germany due to some misunderstanding." That would suit me best and would also be more helpful for my work, which is so urgent just now. If you say any more, somebody might be unnecessarily interested. And please do it right away. Please do not think that I regret having come here. I am very glad to have seen it all and I have learnt a lot. My greatest worry is that I have not seen you and your wife. And now farewell, my dear Paul. May God take care of you and your wife and give you strength and joy for your work and also keep up our friendship as it always has been.

Back in Germany, Bonhoeffer resumed his teaching of Confessing Church ordinants, but in 1940 his work was again dissolved and he became a wandering preacher in the northern provinces. One afternoon while he and Bethge were in Memel, in Prussia, on an evangelical tour, they were seated in a crowded café when they heard on the radio the blast of trumpets that always preceded an important news announcement. This time, it was the fall of France. According to ritual, the broadcast concluded with the singing of the Horst Wessel Song. The customers in the café jumped up jubilantly, raised their right arms, and joined in the singing. Bethge hung back, but then saw that Bonhoeffer not only was on his feet but had his arm up and was singing. Bonhoeffer managed to whisper to Bethge, "Are you mad?" Bethge followed his example, and afterward Bonhoeffer explained, "We mustn't sacrifice ourselves in protest against such ridiculous things. We have to sacrifice ourselves for something far graver." Pastor Bethge knew that whatever hesitation Bonhoeffer might have had about living a life of deception in the name of Christianity had vanished, and that he was now launched on his treasonous career. (Later, it would be called the third and last phase of his life.) By now, Bonhoeffer had come to believe that his service to God could not be divorced from his political beliefs and actions. He knew that if he was captured he would have to lie and deceive and become a part of what he called "the great masquerade of evil;" he believed that under the circumstances this was his duty as a Christian. For a cleric, he held unconventional moral opinions, personal as well as political. He believed that men should live well—should eat, drink, and love well. (Twice, he seems to have considered marriage; the second time —in 1942—he was actually engaged to a nineteen-year-old girl, Maria von Wedemeyer, against the wishes of her mother, who disapproved, at first, because of the pair's difference in age.) In a chapter of a projected book on ethics he wrote:

Love that is really lived does not withdraw from reality to dwell in noble souls secluded from the world. It suffers the reality of the world in all its harshness. The world exhausts its fury against the body of Christ, and the Church must be willing to risk its existence for the sake of the world.

That he had a chance to put this theory into practice was due to the fact that he was still able to escape military duty, though when his pastoral activities were completely suspended in 1940 he was required to report regularly to the police. He would have been conscripted if he had not been taken, as noted earlier, under the protection of the *Abwehr*. Oster's group, which included Hans von Dohnanyi, was known to Britain as the center of the resistance to Hitler, because it supplied the governments of enemy and neutral countries with accurate information regarding Germany's impending invasions of Norway, Denmark, Holland, and Belgium. However, when the fall of these countries brought Churchill to power, the new Prime Minister had immediately proclaimed unconditional surrender as the policy of his government, which, by putting all Germans, whether pro- or anti-Hitler, on an equal footing, had deprived the resisters of any hope that a government made up of Germans who had succeeded in overthrowing Hitler could negotiate an honorable peace. Since Oster's group, early in its existence, had claimed Bonhoeffer for the *Abwehr* and had made him nominally one of its secret agents, partly to put his knowledge of Britain and his connections there to use on behalf of the Resistance, the resisters looked to him, among others, to obtain from the Churchill government some sort of modification of the policy of unconditional surrender. Now he made his cause one with theirs, and this was to have a remarkable effect on his theological outlook.

Bonhoeffer's active participation in the Resistance culminated when he carried out a secret mission at the end of May, 1942, travelling to Sweden, where he met in the little town of Sigtuna a secret agent from Britain, his old, trusted friend the Bishop of Chichester. Bonhoeffer told the Bishop about the size of the Resistance and its need for British support, yet in a sense he undermined his own mission, because he was filled with doubt about whether Britain should, in fact, grant special treatment to any Germans who had managed to liquidate Hitler. For some time, he had been praying for the defeat of Germany, and he had already declared at an ecumenical meeting in Geneva, in 1941, "Only in defeat can we atone for the terrible crimes we have committed against Europe and the world." He now said to the Bishop, almost in Old Testament accents, "There must be punishment by God. We do not want to escape repentance. . . . Christians do not want to escape repentance, or chaos, if it is God's will to bring it upon us. We must take this judgment as Christians." In any event, the Bishop's subsequent entreaties, at home, to support the Resistance fell on deaf ears. He was told merely that the pastors were being "used . . . without their knowledge." But even if England had given the assurances asked, it is debatable whether they would have so stiffened the resolution of the resisters that they might have actually brought about the assassination of Hitler, for Bonhoeffer, who urged assassination, stood in the minority; most Christians could not find any sanction in their religion for such a violent act. Even after 1943, when the Resistance passed into the hands of young staff officers who had the resources to bring about a coup d'état, no coup could be arranged, for the plotters were frustrated not simply by Hitler's uncanny luck but by their own quarrels and ineptitude and by a poor grasp of the political realities.

The S.D., which handled foreign and domestic security for the S.S., had never liked the independence of the *Abwehr*. It eventually got one of the *Abwehr* agents to talk, and as a result, in April, 1943, Bonhoeffer was arrested, though the Gestapo was unable to come up with any charge against him more serious than evasion of military duty. For the next eighteen months, Bonhoeffer was in the military section of Tegel Prison, near Berlin, where he occupied himself in fabricating a defense, by attending meaningless preliminary hearings, by waiting for a trial that never took place, and in writing letters. These centered on two parallel themes—one suggested by his cry, in a poem, "Lord Jesus Christ/Thou wast poor/and in misery, a captive and forsaken as I am," the other embodied in his oblique remark "Talk of a heroic defeat is not heroic, because it means failure to face the future." (Commentators have seen in this remark a warning both to the members of the Resistance and to the German survivors of the two world wars.) That he was able to write at all was due to the special privileges he enjoyed as a prisoner, which were granted him within a few days of his arrival at Tegel, when it became known that General von Hase, the City Commandant of Berlin, was his mother's cousin. His mother or father or Ursula (who now lived next door to them in Marienburger Allee) or Maria von Wedemeyer was permitted each week to leave for him clean clothes, papers, and books, the books being also message-carriers, since, according to a system worked out in advance between the family and Bonhoeffer, words on alternate pages had been marked. Soon Bonhoeffer turned his cell into a small study, and how he adapted himself to his new surroundings is shown in several letters he wrote to his parents in the period that closed with his first Christmas in prison. On August 3rd, he wrote:

I eat and drink very little, and sit quietly at my desk, and in this way manage to work without hindrance. From time to time I refresh both body and soul with your wonderful things.

On August 17th:

Above all, please don't worry over me unduly. . . . Prison life seems to give one a certain detachment from the alarums and excitements of the day.

On August 31st:

I . . . have got quite a lot of writing done. . . . It is quite interesting to watch this gradual process of self-adaptation. I was given a knife and fork to eat with a week ago—a new concession—and they seemed almost unnecessary, it had become so natural to spread bread etc. with a spoon.

And on December 17th:

For a Christian there is nothing peculiarly difficult about Christmas in a prison cell. I daresay it will have more meaning and will be observed with greater sincerity here in this prison than in places where all that survives of the feast is its name. That misery, suffering, poverty, loneliness, helplessness, and guilt look very different to the eyes of God from what they do to man, that God should come down to the very place which men usually abhor, that Christ was born in a stable because there was no room for him in the inn—these are things which a prisoner can understand better than anyone else.

During this period, German defeats on the Western front and the appearance among the resisters of a remarkable officer, Colonel Claus von Stauffenberg, who had lost in the war the use of his left eye, his right hand and forearm, and two fingers of his left hand, made it seem likely that the resisters would be able to assassinate Hitler at last. Indeed, Stauffenberg, on July 20, 1944, went as far as to smuggle a bomb in his briefcase into Hitler's isolated headquarters—the Wolf's Lair, as it was called, nine miles from Rastenburg, set deep in the forest, and surrounded by minefields, barbed wire, electrified fencing, and many security checkpoints—when he went to a staff officers' meeting with Hitler, where Stauffenberg was expected to report on the state of certain divisions in the Reserve Army. He managed to get some privacy to start the time fuse of the bomb, to carry the well-filled briefcase into the conference room—a wooden structure built aboveground and reinforced with concrete—to take his place at Hitler's table, and to slip the briefcase under that table, even arranging it to face Hitler, and then to leave the conference room on the pretext of a telephone call and watch the explosion from a distance of a hundred yards. The cataclysm convinced him that Hitler was dead, so

Stauffenberg confidently helped to put into operation the mechanism worked out by the resisters for wresting power from the Nazis. Hitler, however, though injured, lived, apparently owing to the mere circumstance that an officer in the conference room, in order to get closer to the table, had moved the brief-case slightly so that it faced away from Hitler. He now visited revenge on the plotters. He ordered an exhaustive Gestapo investigation, which, as one of its minor results, turned up some secret papers directly implicating Hans von Dohnanyi, Rüdiger Schleicher, and Klaus and Dietrich Bonhoeffer. All four would have been executed immediately if it were not that Hitler had just come to realize the extent of the conspiracy and wanted further intelligence. As it was, the Gestapo let them live on—they were carted from one prison or camp to another for six wearing months—just on the chance that they should prove of some value to the investigation. In October, Dietrich Bon-hoeffer was transferred from Tegel to a prison in Gestapo Head-quarters, on Prinz Albrechtstrasse, in Berlin, and in February, during the intensive bombing of Berlin, he was taken to Buchenwald, where he apparently made a great impression on Captain S. Payne Best, an agent of the British Secret Service who was interned there as a special prisoner of war and who lived to write, "Bonhoeffer . . . was all humility and sweetness; he always seemed to me to diffuse an atmosphere of happiness, of joy in every smallest event in life, and of deep gratitude for the mere fact that he was alive. There was something dog-like in the look of fidelity in his eyes and his gladness if you showed that you liked him. He was one of the very few men that I have ever met to whom his God was real and ever close to him."

It is part of the charm of Bonhoeffer's letters, which go up almost to his transfer to Buchenwald, that he reveals himself to be absolutely human. One finds him by turns complacent ("I can't help feeling that everything has taken its natural course;

it has all been inevitable, straightforward, directed by a higher Providence"), nostalgic ("I recall those quiet summer evenings in Friedrichsbrunn, then all the different parishes I have worked in, and then all our family occasions, weddings, christenings, and confirmations"), introspective ("I wonder if we have become too rational. When you have deliberately suppressed every desire for so long, it burns you up inside, or else you get so bottled up that one day there is a terrific explosion"), stoical to the point of harshness ("I told him in no uncertain terms what I thought of people who can be very hard on others and make grand speeches about living dangerously, etc., etc., and then crumple up themselves under the slightest test of endurance. . . . I don't believe I find it easy to despise anyone in real trouble, and I have made that perfectly clear, which no doubt made his hair stand on end; but I can only regard that as contempt-ible"), despondent ("I should tell you how my grim exper-iences often follow me into the night, and the only way I can shake them off is by reciting one hymn after another, and that when I wake up it is generally with a sigh, rather than a hymn of praise"), impractical ("The clergy should live solely on the free-will offerings of their congregations"), contradictory ("It's true that the importance of illusion in human life is not to be underestimated, but for the Christian it is essential to have a hope which is based on solid foundations"), serene ("I am going through another spell of finding it difficult to read the Bible. I never know quite what to make of it. I don't feel guilty at all about it, and I know it won't be long before I return to it again with renewed zest"), and, occasionally, prud-ish, snobbish, tasteless, and polemical as well ("When God was driven out of the world, and from the public side of human life, an attempt was made to retain Him at least in the sphere of the 'personal,' the 'inner life,' the private life. And since every man still has a private sphere, it was thought that he was most vulnerable at this point. The secrets known by a man's valet, that is, to put it crudely, the area of his intimate life—from prayer to his sexual life—have become the hunting ground of modern psychotherapists. In this way they resemble, though quite involuntarily, the dirtiest gutter journalists. Think of the newspapers which specialize in bringing to light the most intimate details about prominent people. They practice social, financial, and political blackmail on their victims: the psychotherapists practice religious blackmail. Forgive me, but I cannot say less about them. From the sociological point of view, this is a revolution from below, a revolt of inferiority. Just as the vulgar mentality is never satisfied until it has seen some highly placed personage in his bathing attire, or in other compromising situations, so it is here. There is a kind of malicious satisfaction in knowing that everyone has his weaknesses and nakednesses. In my contacts with the outcasts of society, its pariahs, I have often noticed how mistrust is the dominant motive in their judgments of other people. Every act of a person of high repute, be it never so altruistic, is suspected from the outset. Incidentally, I find such outcasts in all ranks of society. In a flower garden they grub around for the dung on which the flowers grow. The less responsible a man's life, the more easily he falls a victim to this attitude. This irresponsibility and absence of bonds has its counterpart among the clergy in what I should call the 'priestly' snuffing around in the sins of men in order to catch them out. . . . It is the same kind of thing you find in the novels of the last fifty years, which think they have only depicted their characters properly when they have described them in bed, or in films where it is thought necessary to include undressing scenes"). In the last letter included in the book, there is a poignant sentence that might be said to epitomize Bonhoeffer, fated prisoner that he was: "Could I please have some toothpaste and a few coffee beans?"

In the last days of the war, with the American forces moving rapidly across Germany, Bonhoeffer was transferred again and again. The hellish journey started on Tuesday, April 3rd, when Bonhoeffer and fifteen other Buchenwald inmates, including Payne Best, were crowded in a prison van powered by a wood generator, and headed for Weiden, the village nearest Flossenburg. The front part of the van was packed with billets of wood, while the prisoners, with all their luggage, were squeezed into the small back section of the van so tightly that their legs were pushed up against the baggage and their arms pinned to their sides. The van, filled with exhaust fumes, could move only fifteen miles an hour, and had to be stopped every hour in order to refire the generator and clean the flues, and still the engine had to be raced fifteen minutes more before they could set out again. The journey was long and the prisoners had nothing to eat or drink. Bonhoeffer, a smoker, had saved up his scanty ration of tobacco, which he now shared, touching his companions with his generosity and goodness. They reached Weiden on Wednesday, but the Flossenburg camp was too full to receive them; three were admitted the next day, and the rest were again on the road in the van, proceeding southward in search of accommodations. The thirteen inmates spent Thursday night in the Regensburg state prison, five to a cell, but the next day they were sent on again, only to have the van break down on the road and to spend a cold, stormy night among the bomb craters. Saturday, a replacement for the van arrived, a bus with plate-glass windows and upholstered seats and guards with tommy guns. The entire day was spent trying to get the prisoners across the Danube and behind the crumbling German frontier. At last, a pontoon was found which had escaped bombing, and that night they slept in the local schoolhouse of the Bavarian village of Schönberg. The next day was Sunday, April 8th, and Payne Best recounts, "Pastor Bonhoeffer held a little service and spoke to us in a manner which reached the hearts of all, finding just the right words to express the spirit of our imprisonment and the thoughts and resolutions which it had brought. He had hardly finished his last prayer when the door opened and two evil-looking men in civilian clothes came in and said: 'Prisoner Bonhoeffer. Get ready to come with us.' Those words 'come with us'—for all prisoners they had come to mean one thing only—the scaffold. We bade him goodbye—he drew me aside—'This is the end,' he said. 'For me the beginning of life,' and then he gave me a message to give, if I could, to the Bishop of Chichester."

Bonhoeffer was once more on the road. He was driven back to Flossenburg, through the narrow stretch of territory still under German control, and reached the concentration camp that night. The next morning, the camp doctor saw him praying in his cell, and later his Bible and a volume of Goethe in which his name was inscribed were found in the guardroom, among the small belongings of the dead, by the liberating armies, who took possession of Flossenburg within a few days.

The exact circumstances of his death—the manner of his execution, and whether he died at the hands of capricious officers acting on their own or by official order of the Nazi government—remain in doubt. But this uncertainty is important only to those skeptics who would resort to a technicality to deny Bonhoeffer even political martyrdom. Niebuhr wrote soon after Bonhoeffer's death, "The story of Bonhoeffer . . . belongs to the modern Acts of the Apostles. . . . It is safe to say that his life and death will become one of the sources of grace for the new church in a new Germany."

Bonhoeffer's afterlife on this earth begins in what has come to be called the theology of liberation, which was conceived in prison and expounded in the form of letters to Pastor Bethge. Because he was a theologian of distinction who had been alternately Barthian and Bultmannian, there had been those who thought he might be able to effect a sort of synthesis of the thought of the two adversaries: of, on the one hand, accepting the really inaccessible word of God as revealed in the Bible, and, on the other, treating that word existentially—that is, discounting everything in the Bible as mythological except insofar as it speaks to us in the accents of our own time. It was thought that such a conjunction, if it were achieved by him, might give theology a lease on life valid for our century. Since Bonhoeffer's death, the number of theologians who think he might have been able to combine the two schools has increased, and not only have his letters on Barth and Bultmann—which, in a sense, are the core of the theological letters—been scoured for clues to what direction he might have taken if he had been allowed to live but his criticisms of the two men, registered there, are still constantly debated in the theological world. In fact, it is impossible to understand Bonhoeffer's influence without looking at them closely. In one important letter he contends that Barth is still a child of nineteenth-century theology, and Bultmann, at best, perhaps a very reluctant child of the twentieth. He writes to Pastor Bethge:

I expect you remember Bultmann's paper on the demythologizing of the New Testament? My view of it today would be not that he went too far, as most people seem to think, but that he did not go far enough. It is not only the mythological conceptions, such as the miracles, the ascension and the like (which are not in principle separable from the conceptions of God, faith, and so on) that are problematic, but the "religious" conceptions themselves. You cannot, as Bultmann imagines, separate God and miracles, but you do have to be able to interpret and proclaim *both* of them in a "non-religious" sense. . . . What do I mean by "interpret in a religious sense"? In my view, that means to speak on the one hand metaphysically, and on the other individualistically. Neither of these is relevant to the Bible message or to the man of today. . . . Barth was the first theologian to begin the criticism of religion—and that remains his really great merit—but he set in its place the positivist doctrine of revelation which says in effect, "Take it or leave it": Virgin Birth, Trinity or anything else, everything which is an equally significant and necessary part of the whole, which latter has to be swallowed as a whole or not at all. That is not in accordance with the Bible. There are degrees of perception and degrees of significance, i.e., a secret discipline must be reestablished whereby the *mysteries* of the Christian faith are preserved from profanation. The positivist doctrine of revelation makes it too easy for itself, setting up, as in the ultimate analysis it does, a law of faith, and mutilating what is, by the incarnation of Christ, a gift for us. The place of religion is taken by the Church—that is, in itself, as the Bible teaches it should be—but the world is made to depend upon itself and left to its own devices, and that is all wrong.

In another letter he returns to his criticisms of Barth and Bultmann, this time setting them in a much wider historical context and subsuming them under his own ideas. There is hardly a passage in recent theological literature that has received more attention than this one, and the letter deserves to be reproduced almost in its entirety:

I will try to define my position from the historical angle.

The movement beginning about the thirteenth century . . . towards the autonomy of man (under which head I place the discovery of the laws by which the world lives and manages in science, social and political affairs, art, ethics and religion) has in our time reached a certain completion. Man has learned to cope with all questions of importance without recourse to God as a working hypothesis. In questions concerning science, art, and even ethics, this has become an understood thing which one scarcely dares to tilt at any more. But for the last hundred years or so it has been increasingly true of religious questions also: it is becoming evident that everything gets along without "God," and just as well as before. As in the scientific field, so in human affairs generally, what we call "God" is being more and more edged out of life, losing more and more ground.

Catholic and Protestant historians are agreed that it is in this development that the great defection from God, from Christ, is to be discerned, and the more they bring in and make use of God and Christ in opposition to this trend, the more the trend itself considers itself to be anti-Christian. The world which has attained to a realization of itself and of the laws which govern its existence is so sure of itself that we become frightened. False starts and failures do not make the world deviate from the path and development it is following; they are accepted with fortitude and detachment as part of the bargain, and even an event like the present war is no exception. Christian apologetic has taken the most varying forms of opposition to this self-assurance. Efforts are made to prove to a world thus come of age that it cannot live without the tutelage of "God." Even though there has been surrender on all secular problems, there still remain the so-called ultimate questions—death, guilt—on which only "God" can furnish an answer, and which are the reasons why God and the Church and the pastor are needed. Thus we live, to some extent, by these ultimate questions of humanity. But what if one day they no longer exist as such, if they too can be answered without "God"? We have of course the secularized offshoots of Christian theology, the existentialist philosophers and the psychotherapists, who demonstrate to secure, contented, happy mankind that it is really unhappy and desperate, and merely unwilling to realize that it is in severe straits it knows nothing at all about, from which only they can rescue it. Wherever there is health, strength, security, simplicity, they spy luscious fruit to gnaw at or to lay their pernicious eggs in. They make it their object first of all to drive men to inward despair, and then it is all theirs. That is secularized methodism. And whom does it touch? A small number of intellectuals, of degenerates, of people who regard themselves as the most important thing in the world and hence like looking after themselves. The ordinary man who spends his everyday life at work, and with his family, and of course with all kinds of hobbies and other interests too, is not affected. He has neither time nor inclination for thinking about his intellectual despair and regarding his modest share of happiness as a trial, a trouble, or a disaster.

The attack by Christian apologetic upon the adulthood of the world I consider to be in the first place pointless, in the second ignoble, and in the third un-Christian. Pointless, because it looks to me like an attempt to put a grown-up man back into adolescence, i.e., to make him dependent on things on which he is not in fact dependent any more, thrusting him back into the midst of problems which are in fact not problems for him any more. Ignoble, because this amounts to an effort to exploit the weakness of man for purposes alien to him and not freely subscribed to by him. Un-Christian, because for Christ himself is being substituted one particular stage in the religiousness of man, i.e., a human law. Of this more later.

But first a word or two on the historical situation. The question is, Christ and the newly matured world. It was the weak point of liberal theology that it allowed the world the right to assign Christ his place in that world: in the dispute between Christ and the world it accepted the comparatively clement peace dictated by the world. It was its strong point that it did not seek to put back the clock, and genuinely accepted the battle (Troeltsch), even though this came to an end with its overthrow.

Overthrow resulted in capitulation and an attempt at a completely fresh start based on consideration of the Bible and Reformation fundamentals of the faith. . . . Tillich set out to interpret the evolution of the world itself—against its will—in a religious sense, to give it its whole shape through religion. That was very courageous of him, but the world unseated him and went on by itself: he, too, sought to understand the world better than it understood itself, but it felt entirely *mis*understood, and rejected the imputation. (Of course the world does need to be understood better than it understands itself, but not "religiously," as the religious socialists desired.) Barth was the first to realize the mistake that all these efforts (which were all unintentionally sailing in the channel of liberal theology) were making in having as their objective the clearing of a space for religion in the world or against the world.

He called the God of Jesus Christ into the lists against religion, *"pneuma* against *sarx."* That was and is his greatest service (the second edition of his "Epistle to the Romans," in spite of all its neo-Kantian shavings). Through his later "Dogmatics," he enabled the Church to effect this distinction in principle all along the line. It was not that he subsequently, as is often claimed, failed in ethics, for his ethical observations—so far as he has made any—are just as significant as his dogmatic ones; it was that he gave no concrete guidance, either in dogmatics or in ethics, on the non-religious interpretation of theological concepts. There lies his limitation, and because of it his theology of revelation becomes positivist, a "positivism of revelation," as I put it. . . .

Bultmann would seem to have felt Barth's limitations in some way, but he misconstrues them in the light of liberal theology, and hence goes off into the typical liberal reduction process (the "mythological" elements of Christianity are dropped, and Christianity is reduced to its "essence"). I am of the view that the full content, including the mythological concepts, must be maintained. The New Testament is not a mythological garbing of the universal truth; this mythology (resurrection and so on) is the thing itself—but the concepts must be interpreted in such a way as not to make religion a pre-condition of faith (cf. circumcision in St. Paul). Not until that is achieved will, in my opinion, liberal theology be overcome (and even Barth is still dominated by it, though negatively), and, at the same time, the question it raises be genuinely taken up and answered. . . .

The world's coming of age is then no longer an occasion for polemics and apologetics, but it is really better understood than it understands itself, namely on the basis of the Gospel, and in the light of Christ.

The form of Christianity suited to this world-come-of-age is, to use Bonhoeffer's phrase, "religionless Christianity"—an idea so paradoxically expressed that some people find it hopelessly elusive. Indeed, the key fragment in which Bonhoeffer discusses this answer shows him to be only on the verge of formulating the concept himself, and somewhat fearful of its implications. He writes to Pastor Bethge:

You would be surprised and perhaps disturbed if you knew how my ideas on theology are taking shape. This is where I miss you most of all, for there is no one else who could help me so much to clarify my own mind. The thing that keeps coming back to me is, what *is* Christianity, and indeed what *is* Christ, for us today? The time when men could be told everything by means of words, whether theological or simply pious, is over, and so is the time of inwardness and conscience, which is to say the time of religion as such. We are proceeding towards a time of no religion at all: men as they are now simply cannot be religious any more. Even those who honestly describe themselves as "religious" do not in the least act up to it, and so when they say "religious" they evidently mean something quite different. Our whole nineteen-hundred-year-old Christian preaching and theology rests upon the "religious premise" of man. What we call Christianity has always been a pattern— perhaps a true pattern—of religion. But if one day it becomes apparent that this *a priori* "premise" simply does not exist but was an historical and temporary form of human self-expression, i.e., if we reach the stage of being radically without religion—and I think this is more or less the case already, else how is it, for instance, that this war, unlike any of those before it, is not calling forth any "religious" reaction?—what does that mean for "Christianity"?

It means that the linchpin is removed from the whole structure of our Christianity to date, and the only people left for us to light on in the way of "religion" are a few "last survivals of the age of chivalry," or else one or two who are intellectually dishonest. Would they be the chosen few? Is it on this dubious group and none other that we are to pounce, in fervour, pique, or indignation, in order to sell them the goods we have to offer? Are we to fall upon one or two unhappy people in their weakest moment and force upon them a sort of religious coercion?

If we do not want to do this, if we had finally to put down the western pattern of Christianity as a mere preliminary stage to doing without religion altogether, what situation would result for us, for the Church? How can Christ become the Lord even of those with no religion? If religion is no more than the garment of Christianity— and even that garment has had very different aspects at different periods—then what is a religionless Christianity? Barth, who is the only one to have started on this line of thought, has still not proceeded to its logical conclusion, but has arrived at a positivism of revelation which has nevertheless remained essentially a restoration. For the religionless working man, or indeed, man generally, nothing that makes any real difference is gained by that. The questions needing answers would surely be: What is the significance of a

Church (church, parish, preaching, Christian life) in a religionless world? How do we speak of God without religion, i.e., without the temporally influenced presuppositions of metaphysics, inwardness and so on? How do we speak (but perhaps we are no longer capable of speaking on such things as we used to) in secular ᶜashion of God? In what way are we in a religionless and secular sense Christians, in what way are we the *Ekklesia,* "those who are called forth," not conceiving of ourselves religiously as specially favoured, but as wholly belonging to the world? Then Christ is no longer an object of religion, but something quite different indeed and in truth the Lord of the world. Yet what does that signify? What is the place of worship and prayer in an entire absence of religion? Does the secret discipline, or, as the case may be, the distinction (which you have met with me before) between penultimate and ultimate, at this point acquire fresh importance? . . .

I find after all I can carry on writing. The Pauline question whether circumcision is a condition of justification is today, I consider, the question whether religion is a condition of salvation. Freedom from circumcision is at the same time freedom from religion. I often ask myself why a Christian instinct frequently draws me more to the religionless than to the religious, by which I mean not with any intention of evangelizing them, but rather, I might almost say, in "brotherhood." While I often shrink with religious people from speaking of God by name—because that Name somehow seems to me here not to ring true, and I strike myself as rather dishonest (it is especially bad when others start talking in religious jargon: then I dry up completely and I feel somehow oppressed and ill at ease)—with people who have no religion I am able on occasion to speak of God quite openly and as it were naturally. Religious people speak of God when human perception is (often just from laziness) at an end, or human resources fail: it is really always the *Deus ex machina* they call to their aid, either for the so-called solving of insoluble problems or as support in human failure—always, that is to say, helping out human weakness or on the borders of human existence. Of necessity, that can only go on until men can, by their own strength, push those borders a little further, so that God becomes superfluous as a

Deus ex machina. I have come to be doubtful even about talking of "borders of human existence." Is even death today, since men are scarcely afraid of it any more, and sin, which they scarcely understand any more, still a genuine borderline? It always seems to me that in talking thus we are only seeking frantically to make room for God. I should like to speak of God not on the borders of life but at its centre, not in weakness but in strength, not, therefore, in man's suffering and death but in his life and prosperity. On the borders it seems to me better to hold our peace and leave the problem unsolved. Belief in the Resurrection is not the solution of the problem of death. The "beyond" of God is not the beyond of our perceptive faculties. The transcendence of theory based on perception has nothing to do with the transcendence of God. God is the "beyond" in the midst of our life. The Church stands not where human powers give out, on the borders, but in the centre of the village. That is the way it is in the Old Testament, and in this sense we still read the New Testament far too little on the basis of the Old. The outward aspect of this religionless Christianity, the form it takes, is something to which I am giving much thought, and I shall be writing to you about it again soon. It may be that on us in particular, midway between East and West, there will fall an important responsibility.

In short, he defines one paradoxical idea by another—"religion-less Christianity" by "the beyond in our midst." It is somewhat confusing, but one has to remember the circumstances in which Bonhoeffer was writing. In any event, one is held by the voice, as when he grapples with this general theme farther on: "I find it's very slow going trying to work out a non-religious interpretation of Biblical terminology, and it's a far bigger job than I can imagine at the moment."

He continues, almost in an intellectual shorthand:

On the historical side I should say there is *one* great development which leads to the idea of the autonomy of the world. In theology it is first discernible in Lord Herbert of Cherbury, with his assertion that reason is the sufficient instrument of religious knowledge. In ethics it first appears in Montaigne and Bodin with their substitution of moral principles for the ten commandments. In politics, Machiavelli, who emancipates politics from the tutelage of morality, and founds the doctrine of "reasons of state." Later, and very differently, though like Machiavelli tending towards the autonomy of human society, comes Grotius, with his international law as the law of nature, a law which would still be valid, *etsi deus non daretur*. The process is completed in philosophy. On the one hand we have the deism of Descartes, who holds that the world is a mechanism which runs on its own without any intervention of God. On the other hand there is the pantheism of Spinoza, with its identification of God with nature. In the last resort Kant is a deist, Fichte and Hegel pantheists. All along the line there is a growing tendency to assert the autonomy of man and the world.

In natural science the process seems to start with Nicolas of Cusa and Giordano Bruno with their "heretical" doctrine of the infinity of space. The classical cosmos was finite, like the created world of the Middle Ages. An infinite universe, however it be conceived, is self-subsisting *etsi deus non daretur*. It is true that modern physics is not so sure as it was about the infinity of the universe, but it has not returned to the earlier conceptions of its finitude.

There is no longer any need for God as a working hypothesis, whether in morals, politics, or science. Nor is there any need for such a God in religion or philosophy (Feuerbach). In the name of intellectual honesty these working hypotheses should be dropped or dispensed with as far as possible. A scientist or physician who seeks to provide edification is a hybrid.

At this point nervous souls start asking what room there is left for God now. And being ignorant of the answer they write off the whole development which has brought them to this pass. As I said in an earlier letter, various emergency exits have been devised to deal with this situation. To them must be added the *salto mortale* back to the Middle Ages, the fundamental principle of which however is heteronomy in the form of clericalism. [In other words, bowing to ecclesiastical authority.] But that is a counsel of despair, which can be purchased only at the cost of intellectual sincerity. It reminds one of the song:

It's a long way back to the land of childhood
But if only I knew the way!

There isn't any such way, at any rate not at the cost of deliberately
abandoning our intellectual sincerity. The only way is that of
Matthew 18:3, i.e., through repentance, through *ultimate* honesty.
And the only way to be honest is to recognize that we have to
live in the world *etsi deus non daretur*. And this is just what we do
see—before God! So our coming of age forces us to a true recognition of our situation *vis à vis* God. God is teaching us that we
must live as men who can get along very well without him. The
God who is with us is the God who forsakes us (Mark 15:34).
The God who makes us live in this world without using him as
a working hypothesis is the God before whom we are ever standing.
Before God and with him we live without God. God allows
himself to be edged out of the world and on to the cross. God
is weak and powerless in the world, and that is exactly the way,
the only way, in which he can be with us and help us. Matthew
8:17 makes it crystal clear that it is not by his omnipotence that
Christ helps us but by his weakness and suffering.

This is the decisive difference between Christianity and all
religions. Man's religiosity makes him look in his distress to the
power of God in the world; he uses God as a *Deus ex machina*.
The Bible however directs him to the powerlessness and suffering
of God; only a suffering God can help. To this extent we may
say that the process we have described by which the world came
of age was an abandonment of a false conception of God, and a
clearing of the decks for the God of the Bible, who conquers
power and space in the world by his weakness. This must be
the starting point for our "wordly" interpretation.

Two days later, multiplying the paradoxes, he writes:

Man is challenged to participate in the sufferings of God at the
hands of a godless world.
He must therefore plunge himself into the life of a godless
world, without attempting to gloss over its ungodliness with a
veneer of religion or trying to transfigure it. He must live a

"worldly" life and so participate in the suffering of God. He *may* live a worldly life as one emancipated from all false religions and obligations. To be a Christian does not mean to be religious in a particular way, to cultivate some particular form of asceticism (as a sinner, a penitent or a saint) but to be a man. It is not some religious act which makes a Christian what he is but participation in the suffering of God in the life of the world.

This is *metanoia*. It is not in the first instance bothering about one's own needs, problems, sins, and fears, but allowing oneself to be caught up in the way of Christ, into the Messianic event, and thus fulfilling Isaiah 53. . . . This being caught up into the Messianic suffering of God in Jesus Christ takes a variety of forms in the New Testament. It appears in the call to discipleship, in Jesus' table fellowship with sinners, [and] in conversions in the narrower sense of the word. . . . All that is common between them is their participation in the suffering of God in Christ. That is their faith. There is nothing of religious asceticism here. The religious act is always something partial, faith is always something whole, an act involving the whole life. Jesus does not call men to a new religion, but to life. What is the nature of that life, that participation in the powerlessness of God in the world? More about that next time, I hope.

Just one more point for today. When we speak of God in a non-religious way, we must not gloss over the ungodliness of the world, but expose it in a new light. Now that it has come of age, the world is more godless, and perhaps it is for that very reason nearer to God than ever before.

And three days later still:

During the last year or so I have come to appreciate the "worldliness" of Christianity as never before. The Christian is not a *homo religiosus,* but a man, pure and simple, just as Jesus was man, compared with John the Baptist anyhow. I don't mean the shallow this-worldliness of the enlightened, of the busy, the comfortable or the lascivious. It's something much more profound than that, something in which the knowledge of death and resurrection is ever present. . . . Later I discovered and am still discovering up to this very moment that it is only by living completely in this world that one learns to believe. One must abandon every attempt to make something of oneself, whether it be a saint, a converted sinner, a churchman (the priestly type, so-called!), a righteous man or an unrighteous one, a sick man or a healthy one. This is what I mean by worldliness—taking life in one's stride, with all its duties and problems, its successes and failures, its experiences and helplessness. It is in such a life that we throw ourselves utterly in the arms of God and participate in his sufferings in the world and watch with Christ in Gethsemane. That is faith, that is *metanoia,* and that is what makes a man and a Christian (cf. Jeremiah 45).

When he leaves paradoxes behind, it is only to turn to metaphors, it seems. The results, however, are more convincing, since the imagery, being emotional, tends to add a personal quality to his views, making one think that the problems themselves, however great the efforts to solve them, were intractable. One feels as he trips over a paradox that the stumbling block may be the very subject that the paradox is trying to resolve. One particular passage comes to mind:

There is always a danger of intense love destroying what I might call the "polyphony" of life. What I mean is that God requires that we should love him eternally with our whole hearts, yet not so as to compromise or diminish our earthly affections but as a kind of *cantus firmus* to which the other melodies of life provide the counterpoint. Earthly affection is one of these contrapuntal themes, a theme which enjoys an autonomy of its own. Even the Bible can find room for the Song of Songs, and one could hardly have a more passionate and sensual love than is there portrayed (see 7:6). It is a good thing that that book is included in the Bible as a protest against those who believe that Christianity stands for the restraint of passion (is there any example of such restraint anywhere in the Old Testament?). Where the ground bass is firm and clear, there is nothing to stop the counterpoint from being developed to the utmost of its limits. Both ground bass and counterpoint are "without confusion and yet distinct," in the words of the Chalcedonian formula, like Christ in his divine and human natures. Perhaps the importance of polyphony in music lies in the fact that it is a musical reflection of this Christological truth, and that it is therefore an essential element in the Christian life.

But it would be unfair to leave the impression that precision always plays, one is tempted to say, second fiddle to metaphor or paradox. In a letter concerning the doctrine of salvation, he writes:

To resume our reflections on the Old Testament. Unlike the other Oriental religions the faith of the Old Testament is not a religion of salvation. Christianity, it is true, has always been regarded as a religion of salvation. But isn't this a cardinal error, which divorces Christ from the Old Testament and interprets him in the light of the myths of salvation? Of course it could be urged that under Egyptian and, later, Babylonian influence, the idea of salvation became just as prominent in the Old Testament—e.g., Deutero-Isaiah. The answer is, the Old Testament speaks of *historical* redemption, i.e., redemption on this side of death, whereas the myths of salvation are concerned to offer men deliverance from death. Israel is redeemed out of Egypt in order to live before God on earth. The salvation myths deny history in the interests of an eternity after death. Sheol and Hades are no metaphysical theories but images which imply that the past, while it still exists, has only a shadowy existence in the present. It is said that the distinctive feature of Christianity is its proclamation of the resurrection, hope, and that this means the establishment of a genuine religion of salvation, in the sense of release from this world. The emphasis falls upon the far side of the boundary drawn by death. But this seems to me to be just the mistake and the danger. Salvation means salvation from cares and need, from fears and longing, from sin and death into a better world beyond the grave. But is this really the distinctive feature of Christianity as proclaimed in the Gospels and St. Paul? I am sure it is not. The difference between the Christian hope of resurrection and a mythological hope is that the Christian hope sends a man back to his life on earth in a wholly new way which is even more sharply defined than it is in the Old Testament.

The Christian, unlike the devotees of the salvation myths, does not need a last refuge in the eternal from earthly tasks and difficulties. But like Christ himself ("My God, my God, why hast thou forsaken me?") he must drink the earthly cup to the lees, and only in his doing that is the crucified and risen Lord with him, and he crucified and risen with Christ. This world must not be prematurely written off. In this the Old and New Testaments are at one. Myths of salvation arise from human experiences of the boundary situation. Christ takes hold of a man in the centre of his life.

Wherever one pauses over a paradox, a metaphor, or a concrete example in the theological letters, one is faced with conclusions so unmistakably this-worldly in their implications that in the end it sometimes becomes difficult to remember that what is under discussion is Christianity.

It was to find out how Bonhoeffer was regarded in Germany twenty years after his death that I paid my visit to Pastor Bethge, who turned out to live in Rengsdorf, a village so small that it had to be identified as near another town, Neuwied. One fine winter morning, I arrived by train in Koblenz, where I found Pastor Bethge waiting on the station platform. A fifty-five-year-old man, six feet one inch tall, with an open and extraordinarily friendly face and graying black hair, he was dressed in a pastor's black suit under a black overcoat, and he was carrying a gray hat in one hand and a blue airline bag under the other arm. Even so, he insisted on carrying my luggage. As we walked through the station, he began telling me about his wife.

"My wife, Renate, is going to pick us up," Pastor Bethge

said. "She is driving back from Bonn, where she attends the university. She is studying psychology there." As though to forestall any questions, he went on, "She was unable to complete her education, because of the war. She wouldn't go to the university before the children had grown up, because she wanted to be a good mother. This is typical Bonhoeffer, *ja?* That a mother should give herself completely to her children. She is a daughter of Rüdiger Schleicher and Ursula. Renate had seen the Bonhoeffer widows. They felt lost after their husbands died. That's why Renate wanted to do psychology, to be something in her own right, *ja?*"

By now we were standing on the pavement outside the station. An Opel Rekord drew up, and out jumped a young-looking woman with blond hair and blue eyes. She shook my hand energetically. We all got in, Mrs. Bethge behind the wheel again.

"I hope you are comfortable," Pastor Bethge said.

"We bought this car second-hand last year to go to Berlin for the twentieth anniversary of the July plot," Mrs. Bethge said.

"Until then we had never tried to interest our children in the Resistance movement," Pastor Bethge said. "But in Berlin our children met the children of men who had died in the German Resistance. They got so interested that later two of them went to France on their own to a meeting of the families of members of the French and German Resistance."

I asked how many children they had.

"Three," Mrs. Bethge said. "On the way home, we will pass through Neuwied. Our two daughters go to school there. Gabriele, who is nineteen, is going to make an *Abitur* this week. Sabine is the younger one—she is eighteen."

"Sabine is named after Dietrich's twin sister," Pastor Bethge said. "We named our son, who is twenty-one now, after Dietrich. He was our son's godfather, and the baptism sermon in the 'Letters and Papers' was for him. Dietrich is at Christ Church,

Oxford. Before that, he was in Westminster. He was admitted to the school with the help of the Bishop of Chichester."

In due course, we reached Rengsdorf bei Neuwied, an ancient village deep in clean snow; it seemed that the plow was used only on the main roads. Above, there was an extraordinarily bright and warm sun.

I remarked on how peaceful things were.

"In Germany, every pastor should go into retreat periodically for one or two weeks and take a refresher course in some theological subject," Pastor Bethge said. "Rengsdorf is a place of retreat, and next week we are having a conference on the New Testament here. I teach the pastors studying in Rengsdorf. This means I have to read all the books on religious matters that come out, and this I cannot do, because of the work I am doing on Dietrich's biography "

"Rengsdorf has a population of only about two thousand," Mrs. Bethge said. "But it has been rather lively lately, because the burgomaster has got the government to recognize it officially as a resort. People can come here now on social security."

Pastor Bethge pointed out the remains of an old wall, to our left, and remarked, "That's a Roman wall. Now we are leaving civilization." Indeed, there were now woods all around us.

Presently, we pulled up in front of a small house and got out. Inside, the house was snug and friendly; there were low ceilings and plenty of heat.

We had lunch right away. At the dining table, Mrs. Bethge talked with spirit about the Bonhoeffer family. "The Bonhoeffers see more of each other than many families do," she said, "and are very much alike."

"Michael, Suzanne's son, however, is in London," Pastor Bethge said. "He has now taken up composing. He telephoned the other day and asked for a copy of one of Dietrich's poems, which he wanted to set to music. The piece was commissioned for a Dietrich Bonhoeffer anniversary celebration in London, which is to be attended by the Archbishop of Canterbury and Bishop Robinson. The celebration will take place in St. Mary le Bow Church."

Mrs. Bethge, who was serving soup, said to me, "Your soup spoon is from the Bonhoeffer house. The family was so large that each of us children got one or two things."

Two blond, blue-eyed girls, both dressed in yellow sweaters and yellow skirts, joined us. They were Gabriele and Sabine.

"How is the sewing of your very pink dress?" Pastor Bethge asked Sabine, and he explained to me that this was her first venture in dressmaking.

"It's not a *very* pink dress, Papa," Sabine said shyly but firmly.

"Gabriele plays the violin," Pastor Bethge told me proudly. "Neuwied is a very small town, but it has three orchestras, and Gabriele has played in all three of them."

"Her playing has been reviewed in the Neuwied newspaper," Mrs. Bethge added with a smile.

"It's a terribly bad paper," Gabriele said with an intellectual air. "Besides, the reviewer was my violin teacher at school."

At a word from Mrs. Bethge, the two girls swiftly removed the soup plates and brought in platters of English cheeses and German liver sausages, a large bowl of pea salad, and a basket filled with black bread. We all served ourselves. There was some discussion about whether Gabriele would be called to sit for an oral examination the following day. Everyone except Gabriele felt she had done so well in her studies that she would be exempt from that part of the *Abitur*.

"I don't like the thought of an oral examination at all," Gabriele said. "They can ask you anything they want."

"The oral part of the pastoral examination was all that got me through," Pastor Bethge said.

"But you like talking," Gabriele said.

"When we first came back to Rengsdorf, we were very much

worried about the education of our girls," Mrs. Bethge said. "I called the headmaster of the school in Neuwied and told him that our girls had spent many years in English public schools and had done well there, but that they were not very good in German. I said I thought they would be able to pick up German in about half a year. The headmaster said, 'I think two years.' You see, in England, if you have deficiencies, they try to help you overcome them, but in Germany it's not like that."

"England is far more democratic," Pastor Bethge put in. "And the teachers there always stress a student's good qualities. In Germany, the teachers notice your bad points."

"The headmaster did finally agree to see the two girls," Mrs. Bethge resumed. "And then, when I told him that my father and my uncles had died in concentration camps, he immediately consented to take Gabriele and Sabine."

"He's the best history teacher I've ever had, Mama," Sabine said. "When he tells about Nazism, he gets so angry that he stamps his foot."

"The headmaster talks too much about Nazism," Mrs. Bethge continued. "Because you know how children are—whatever their elders say, they tend to resent it. I don't understand the Germans today. When I first came here, I had difficulty finding a cleaning woman, and I called on a neighbor to ask if she knew of anyone. Before I left, she said to me, 'If my father had lived through the war, he would have been hanged at Nuremberg.' Imagine that— boasting to me about her Nazi father! I told her that my father and my uncles had died in the Resistance. She didn't even know there had been a German Resistance, and asked me to lend her some of my books on it. She returned the books within a week."

"I'm sure she didn't read them, Mama," Gabriele said.

"Oh, I don't know—one ought to be charitable," Mrs. Bethge said, and continued, "And when we were in London, a German who had been in a concentration camp came up to me and said,

'Renate, I wish I had been as clever as your Uncle Dietrich and got myself killed in the camp. Then I would have hostels and churches named after me today.' "

"As though he had got himself killed! How awful, Mama!" Gabriele said.

"But we also have a friend who was in a concentration camp," said Pastor Bethge. "In a sermon I gave once I mentioned the word 'Pharisee,' and he did not like my Christian devaluation of this group of Jewish leaders. He thought it sounded anti-Semitic."

The girls cleared the table quickly and brought in a very fluffy mousse.

"This mousse is just the kind of thing a Bonhoeffer *would* come up with," Pastor Bethge said, with anticipation. "Something fantastically complicated when there is a guest in the house."

Pastor and Mrs. Bethge now started talking about how troubled they were by what was going on in Germany just then. Erhard's government was asking for special powers in case the East Germans or the Russians should take it into their heads to violate the West German borders, as though, if that happened, West Germany could not rely on the protection of the French, the English, the Americans—the whole free world. To the Bethges, Erhard's emergency powers were reminiscent of Hitler. They said that the former Defense Minister Franz Josef Strauss had ridden rough-shod over police and journalists, and that some of the younger generation, forgetting Hitler's part in the war and the persecution of the Jews, now talked of his achievements—full employment and the building of the *Autobahnen*.

The girls had disappeared again, and now the dining room suddenly vibrated with a hum. Pastor Bethge and Mrs. Bethge stood up. "That's the dishwasher—my present to Renate when she decided to start going to the university," Pastor Bethge said. "Let's go into the living room."

In the living room were a grand piano, a clavichord, and some pieces of Biedermeier furniture. "I can't drink port," Pastor Bethge said, making himself comfortable in a chair next to Mrs. Bethge. "It's very sad, but I'm a little asthmatic, and wine exacerbates the condition. I do, however, smoke a cigar, and if you'll allow me, I'll light one." He lit a large cigar, and continued, with a long, contented sigh, "Do you remember a letter from prison in which Dietrich says he imagines us sitting together as we used to, smoking, occasionally strumming a tune on the clavichord, and discussing the day's events? This was the clavichord he was talking about. We bought it together."

Going over to the clavichord, Pastor Bethge played a few notes on it. It was painfully out of tune. "We don't use it much," he said. "In England, some time back, I was pastor of the same German church in London that Dietrich served. We had a very damp Victorian house, and when we brought the piano back to this house from there, it sounded horrible. It took a year to get acclimated." He talked of how difficult it was in any case to tune an instrument well, and said that one had to master the old organ builders' technique of tuning strings (or pipes) in pairs, one a little flatter than the other, for maximum resonance.

"We all have musical evenings here, but this room isn't very good for music," Gabriele said, bringing in coffee. "The ceilings are too low. Once, when my brother Dietrich was here, he put a loudspeaker under the clavichord, so it wouldn't be drowned out by his cello."

"Dietrich is a very keen cellist," Mrs. Bethge said. "He plays in several orchestras at Oxford."

After coffee, Pastor Bethge took me into his study. (From upstairs came the sound of Gabriele confidently practicing the violin.) Around the walls were the books that I had come to associate with German theologians—the collected works of Nietzsche and of Kant, of Troeltsch, of Emil Brunner, of Karl Barth—and, surprisingly, Cervantes and Balzac were also there. Bultmann was not.

"These were Dietrich's books," said Pastor Bethge.

"No Bultmann?" I asked.

"In Dietrich's academic period, Bultmann wasn't of so much interest, *ja?*" Pastor Bethge replied. "Later, Dietrich owned a Bultmann, but during his imprisonment it was destroyed in the house of his fiancée, in the Neumark, east of Berlin. He left his books to me in his will." The pastor turned to his desk, which was covered with untidy stacks of papers. From the top of one stack he handed me a copy of the will, which was in the form of a letter, and was dated November 23, 1943. It read, in part:

DEAR EBERHARD: After yesterday's air raid I think it is good to let you know what testamentary dispositions I have made in the event of my death. . . . You will, so I hope, read this with your own peculiar lack of sentimentality. . . . You will get my whole library, including all the untheological things, and the grand piano, the car, the motorcycle, the money in the postal-savings account, one of the icons, the doctor-books, the Rembrandt Bible . . . the carpet in the house of Heinz Lang, the Chinese carpet. . . . All you need of my clothes you will get anyhow.

I asked Pastor Bethge how he and Bonhoeffer had happened to become such close friends.

"I met Dietrich in 1935, in Finkenwalde," Pastor Bethge said. "He somehow got interested in me. Perhaps he saw there was something in me that wasn't developed but that he could develop. I spent holidays with him. We couldn't have been more different. He came from a very good family. I was the son of a simple country parson, and my father had died at an early age. In Germany, you know, becoming a pastor is something that lower-middle-class people do. The son of a worker might become a pastor in order to take a step up; his eldest son might also become a pastor, and in the third or fourth generation, if the family had saved enough money, one of the grandsons might go to a university and become a doctor or a professor. Dietrich was the son of a well-known doctor. His becoming a pastor was a step down. If it hadn't been for the war, I wonder how I would have married into the Bonhoeffer family. Even so, I was told later that there was quite a lot of discussion between Renate's parents over whether I could be permitted to marry her. Dietrich and I were different in so many ways. Having been brought up in a simple country parson's home, I believed that sleeping pills were bad, *ja?* But Dietrich always carried all kinds of powders and compounds in his shaving bag. He never thought that taking pills was somehow unhealthy. I suppose he got into the habit of taking medicine from his mother. She was a doctor's wife, and she had great confidence in medicine. When I was ill, Dietrich would dose me with the authority of a doctor. He himself took sleeping pills freely, but I still get a hangover from a sleeping pill. Recently, Gabriele and her brother went to Greece, and when they came back Gabriele told me that her brother had handed out pills to everybody."

Pastor Bethge laughed, and went on, "When I first met Dietrich at Finkenwalde, I had no self-confidence. Dietrich, for his part, sometimes felt he had taken advantage of me. He knew I was a weaker person than he. He once wrote from prison asking me to forgive him for the mental violence he might have done me. From the time I met Dietrich, demands were made on me for which I had no preparation, *ja?*"

I asked him what he meant.

"I am now writing a biography of Dietrich, in two volumes," he said. "But I feel that I haven't the education or the experience to do it. I am not an academic type of theologian—I have no doctorate—and this biography is the first full-length piece of writing I have ever tried to do. I know so little about writing that I wrote my first draft on both sides of the paper, so when I came to do my second draft, I couldn't cut it up. Well, all the material

I have on Dietrich will be in the biography. It won't be a book that anybody will be able to read, but from it some future person will be able to write the real biography."

Pastor Bethge laughed. It was a free, boisterous, English kind of laugh, different from any other laugh I had heard in Germany. He went on, "Goethe, you know, had his secretary, J. P. Eckermann. Every decent German has the 'Conversations with Goethe,' by Eckermann, on his shelf. It is not read very much now, but Eckermann did put down all the golden words of Goethe—what he said when he was cleaning his teeth in the morning, what he said over breakfast, what he said just before he went to sleep. Well, I could never be an Eckermann, but Dietrich, late in his life, did begin to make jokes about my writing his biography. He would say, 'One day perhaps you will write my biography, and so you should know this.' But I didn't take any notes on Dietrich's golden words when he was alive."

I asked Pastor Bethge what had actually got him started on the biography.

"When Dietrich died, he left an unfinished book of ethics, which I regarded as his last will and testament," he said. "I finished it, and after that I came across all these papers of Dietrich's in my desk. His parents had kept practically everything he wrote them, and they had given everything to me. The surviving members of his family have since given me most of his letters to them. I am now missing the letters he wrote to the two girls he was in love with, and I may be missing many things more."

Pastor Bethge showed me some of the papers on his desk. There were the originals of a number of Bonhoeffer's prison letters; they were written very small, as if to make the most of a sheet of paper. Many of them were in pencil, but a few were in ink. There were some soiled pieces of paper scribbled on both sides with notes for his defense. Almost all the papers lying on Pastor Bethge's desk were dog-eared and discolored by age or damp. Some of them were held together with tape, and others were so mutilated that they had had to be placed between celluloid covers. Moreover, many of the sheets were marked up, crossed out, underlined, or otherwise annotated in another, almost illegible hand. It was Bethge's. The effect was that of a palimpsest.

"I'm afraid the damp got into these papers," Pastor Bethge said. "When I was in the Army, I used to send all the letters I received from Dietrich to my mother and Renate, who would bury them in the garden; we didn't want Himmler's Gestapo to find them. Paul Lehmann visited me once and asked me what I was doing with the letters. That was when I first realized that I might have something valuable. Later, I collected a third of them for the 'Letters and Papers from Prison.' But when I was putting the 'Letters and Papers from Prison' together, I marked them up for the secretary, *ja?* I should have had them copied first, but I didn't realize what a great treasure I had. The 'Letters and Papers from Prison' came out in a very small edition, but Gerhard Ebeling, in Switzerland, and Helmut Thielicke, in Hamburg, gave it good reviews. Professor Ronald Gregor Smith, who was then the director of the Student Christian Movement Press, and who had always been interested in Bonhoeffer, immediately decided to publish the 'Letters and Papers from Prison' in England. I was surprised by its success. I began getting invitations to speak on Dietrich."

I asked Pastor Bethge how the biography was going.

"It gets longer and longer," he said. "The first few pages are going to be a sort of verbal portrait of him."

I asked what it would be like.

"It will go something like this," he said. "Dietrich was a tall man, but he looked a little too heavy for his legs. His head was big, so although his shoulders were broad, they didn't seem so. He had a broad forehead, which made his nose seem shorter than it actually was. His lips were full, and always gave the impression that he was savoring good food. His appearance of heaviness was misleading. He was actually very athletic. In fact, his physical movements were nervous and quick, and he talked like a machine gun. You heard Renate talk. She talks exactly like Dietrich, and she has his laugh. As a person, he was very restless, *ja?* He worked with great concentration—what takes me twenty-four hours he could do in three. For this reason, he had time to do many different things."

Because the books on the Resistance were obscure about the size of Bonhoeffer's role in the conspiracy, I asked Pastor Bethge about it.

"In 1940, Dietrich only knew about the plot, *ja?*" Pastor Bethge said. "Of course, after the July attempt in 1944, any knowledge of a conspiracy was enough to get you hanged. Actually, Dietrich was only connected with the *Abwehr,* and that was just one place out of many all over Germany where resisters were making plans. He never considered murdering Hitler himself, nor did anyone ever suggest that he should, be-cause in the last analysis everything depended on technique, and Dietrich didn't know how to hold a gun. He didn't have a uni-form, and no one who wasn't in uniform was allowed near Hit-ler. In fact, there was no practical way that Dietrich himself could have assassinated Hitler, *ja?* The matter did come up once, hypothetically, and he told me that he would murder Hitler if he could."

I then broached a question that detractors of Bonhoeffer in the Church sometimes asked—whether he was Christian, in any traditional sense.

"For Dietrich, the main thing about Christ was that He was defenseless," Pastor Bethge said. "Dietrich's favorite quotation from the Bible was 'My God, my God, why hast thou forsaken me?' On the Cross, Christ did not have even the protection of God. This was the ultimate defenselessness."

"But did this insight and the ideas contained in 'Letters and Papers' amount to a new theology?" I asked.

"It depends on who it is you are talking to," Pastor Bethge replied. "Karl Barth still won't allow his students to write a doctorate on Dietrich's last period, because it's 'fragmentary,' he says—although he himself, in a sense, opened the door to the Death of God movement when he made Christ the unique and final revelation, and ruled out any metaphysical speculation about God. The Church in Germany still feels very uncomfortable at any mention of Dietrich's name, *ja?* They wish that Bonhoeffer hadn't dirtied his hands with politics."

With amusement, Pastor Bethge gave me a few examples of this unease. When the pastor and people of Flossenburg put up a plaque to commemorate Bonhoeffer, the late Lutheran Bishop of Munich, Hans Meiser, refused to have anything to do with the dedication, on the ground that Bonhoeffer was a political casualty, not a Christian martyr. Then again, in Hanover, the Church government, under its president, Bishop Hanns Lilje, had refused to let a church be named after Bonhoeffer, on the ground that it had to wait a hundred years before declaring anyone a martyr. Pastor Bethge then said he would like to quote a sentence or two from a message commemorating the martyrs which was sent out by the Church administration on the first anniversary of the July plot. Putting on his glasses, he rummaged through the papers on his desk, found the message, and read it, pausing to laugh and repeat phrases that seemed to disavow Bonhoeffer's martyrdom—though he was not mentioned in the message by name—because of his political role and his advocacy of the assassination: " 'Our eyes are set on . . . martyrs in the full'—full!—'sense of the word. . . . We would like to name one, Vicar Paul Schneider'—he didn't engage in politics and so he was the kind of martyr the Church can understand—'and there are other'—other!—'ones who tried to get a different government for our people before the last German town was ruined. . . . The Church of Jesus can never justify an attempt on a human life no matter what the purpose was'—justify!"

Putting down the paper, Pastor Bethge went on, "Even a sculptor who was doing a bust of Bonhoeffer for a school doesn't understand how Bonhoeffer could have done the things he did. The sculptor asked, 'How is it possible that Bonhoeffer, who was a theologian, could take part in an attempt on a human life?'"

Pastor Bethge then handed me what he said was the choicest example of all. It consisted of a letter from the minister of the town of Bielefeld and a reply from Dietrich Bonhoeffer's father:

Bielefeld, 1/4/1948

DEAR MRS. BONHOEFFER,

On behalf of the Conference of Communal Ministers of Bielefeld, I take the liberty of addressing the following request to you. The local council has decided, as per motion of the Social Democratic parliamentary group, to name one of the streets "Bonhoeffer Street" after your late husband, as part of the change of name of a goodly number of streets. A number of people were selected who had been victims of National Socialism, including two ministers, our brother Schneider-Dickenschied and your husband. We, the ministers of our town, are seriously concerned about both names, because we would not like to see our brethren in office, who were killed because of their faith, equated with "political" martyrs. Since we have no say in government decisions, as the town parliament is ruled by a Socialist majority, we ask you—if you agree with us—to write to the chief mayor of our town (Ludebeck, Social Democrat), voicing your objection to the naming of a street after your husband, and to deny permission.

Very sincerely yours,
HAMMERSCHMIDT, Minister

Karl Bonhoeffer replied:

2/11/1948

DEAR REVEREND,

Only yesterday did I receive your kind letter of 1/4. There is a misunderstanding, inasmuch as my son was not married. Therefore I have to answer your letter.

My son Dietrich would not have cared about having a street named after him. On the other hand, I am convinced that it would not be his desire to dissociate himself from the political victims killed, as he had been with them in prison and in concentration camps for years. Therefore, I would rather not protest against the decision of the town council, particularly since the choice of the two ministers seems to indicate that the parliament made its selection without consideration of political position.

With respectful regards, I remain,

Very sincerely yours,

KARL BONHOEFFER, Privy Councillor

"Of course, in those days Socialist more or less meant agnostic and atheist, too," Bethge observed.

I asked him how, in fact, Bonhoeffer would have justified his conduct, and if it was true that in Hitler's time the only Christian martyrdom was political martyrdom.

"An Italian professor once asked Dietrich himself a similar question," Pastor Bethge said. "Dietrich said that if he were walking down the Kurfürstendamm, in Berlin, or Oxford Street, in London, and he saw a madman driving a car, he wouldn't just stand there on the pavement. He wouldn't say to himself, 'I am a pastor. I'll just wait to bury the dead afterward.' His responsibility as a human being would come before any Christian commandment; in fact, killing the madman might become his duty as a Christian."

"But, in any event, do the Protestants have a tradition of martyrs?" I asked.

"Martyrs went out during the Reformation, with the Calendar of Saints and other Catholic practices, it's true," Pastor Bethge said. "The German Evangelical Church doesn't believe in making much of certain individuals, putting them between God and man. But, for my part, I like the Anglicans. They have a tradition of great lives, and in every church you go to, there's a little grave commemorating someone. There is going to be no special recognition by the Church in Germany even of the twentieth anniversary of Dietrich's death. But I've been invited to the Dietrich Bonhoeffer anniversary celebration in London, for which Michael is composing that piece. Both Robinson and I are to speak, and our speeches will be broadcast all over Europe."

And, finally, I asked which Pastor Bethge considered more important—Bonhoeffer's life or his theology.

"Ah, that is a very interesting point," he said. "I think the two were closely connected, but I, since I am not an academic type of theologian, would say his life."

I spent the night in one of Rengsdorf's two inns, and the next day I returned to the Bethge house to learn the results of Gabriele's examination and to say goodbye. I found Pastor Bethge in his study. He was on the telephone, saying excitedly, *"Ach so. . . . Ach so. . . . Ach so. . . . Ach so."* When he hung up, he told me, "That was the headmaster's wife. Everyone in the class had to sit for the orals except her daughter and Gabriele. They were excused because they had done so well on their written papers." With his free laugh, he added, "We gave Gabriele a sleeping pill last night. It was wasted."

There was a fumbling at the study door. Pastor Bethge opened it, and in came Mrs. Bethge, carrying a large silver tray with coffee and tea, a collection of wine and spirits, soda water, cocktail glasses, a shaker, and an ice bucket. Sabine came in behind her. "Ah," Pastor Bethge said, standing back. "When a guest comes, everything belongs to him. Renate will break up any conversation just to be hospitable."

"It's nothing," Mrs. Bethge said, and she slid the tray firmly onto the desk, scattering the precious papers.

Pastor Bethge told them the good news about Gabriele, which they received with great enthusiasm. He explained to me, "Now Gabriele can go to the University of Bonn and study medicine. Bonn has a very good clinic, because, thanks to the presence of

Adenauer and other important people, some of the best doctors have been assembled in the capital. After speaking at Dietrich Bonhoeffer House in Bonn last December, I talked to some people there about taking Gabriele in, and they agreed to. That's very good, because it will enable her to live close to the clinic."

I accepted a glass of sherry from Pastor Bethge. Mrs. Bethge settled herself in a chair and poured out three cups of tea.

"Papa, is this Uncle Dietrich's school report?" Sabine asked, picking up a piece of paper from the desk. "He got only a couple of 'Very Good's. The rest of his marks were average or below average. My report is better than his."

"Perhaps it was just a bad year," Pastor Bethge said.

There were footsteps in the hall, and Gabriele came in, looking very formal in a long-sleeved black dress. She was roundly embraced and then was presented with opera glasses and a china cup. She took all the fuss quite casually.

"The cup is so that she can begin a hope chest," Pastor Bethge explained to me, beaming.

"Papa, do you know what?" Gabriele said. "The burgomaster's daughter, who was doing history, was given a passage from Dietrich Bonhoeffer on civil courage to comment upon." (The passage, I learned later, was from an essay in "Letters and Papers" which he had sent to a few of his friends as a Christmas present in 1942, and which contained sentences like "The last ten years have produced a rich harvest of bravery and self-sacrifice, but hardly any civil courage, even among ourselves. . . . In the course of a long history we Germans have had to learn the necessity and the power of obedience. . . . Who can deny that in obedience, duty, and calling we Germans have again and again excelled in bravery and self-sacrifice? But the German has preserved his freedom—what nation has talked so passionately of freedom as we have, from Luther to the idealists?—by seeking deliverance from his own will through service to the community. . . . Inevitably, he was convicted of a fundamental failure: he could not see that in certain circumstances free and responsible action might have to take precedence over duty and calling. . . . Civil courage . . . can only grow out of the free responsibility of free men. Only now are we Germans beginning to discover the meaning of free responsibility. It depends upon a God who demands bold action as the free response of faith, and who promises forgiveness and consolation to the man who becomes a sinner in the process.")

Mrs. Bethge, Sabine, and Gabriele left us in order to prepare a small luncheon party to celebrate Gabriele's success. Three of her school friends were going to join her, they explained, and although a bakery was supplying the cake, there was quite a lot of cooking to be done.

"Now I would like to ask you a question," Pastor Bethge said when the others had gone. "I don't know how to finish my biography of Dietrich. I have three documents with which I can close it. One is a letter from Dietrich's father to a colleague in Boston; it was the first letter he could get out of Germany after the war. Another is a letter that Dietrich's eldest brother, Karl Friedrich, wrote to his children while he was sitting in his bombed laboratory in Leipzig. He didn't know what had happened to his brothers and brothers-in-law, and he didn't know what would happen to him, so he wrote a letter to his children, in order that they might know all he could tell them." Pastor Bethge broke off, and remained silent for a moment. He resumed, "Then, there is a letter that Hans von Dohnanyi sent to his wife after she had brought him some diphtheria germs, so that he could infect himself and stop the questioning. Karl Bonhoeffer and Karl Friedrich have since died, too."

I read over the three documents. The Dohnanyi letter, dated March 8, 1945, read, in part:

You can hardly imagine how my heart was beating yesterday when I noticed the red-capped cup emerging from the suitcase. . . . The misery around me is so great that I would throw away that

little bit of life, if it were not for all of *you*. . . . I am quite sure
I would lie down with the feeling that this is salvation not only
for me but for many others, too, whose cause is connected with
mine. . . . I took the diphtheria swab into my mouth right away
and chewed it thoroughly. . . . I *must* get out of here and manage
to get into a hospital, *so that I cannot be examined any further!*
[His italics.]

The second one, a letter from Karl Bonhoeffer to Dr. Joss-
mann, in Boston, read, in part:

10/8/45

Dear Colleague:

I was most delighted to receive your regards through your
neighbor and to learn that you are doing all right over there and
that you are engaged in an interesting activity. I understand that
you were told about the sad events we experienced—we lost
two sons (Dietrich, the theologian, and Klaus, Chief Syndikus
of the Lufthansa) and two sons-in-law (. . . Schleicher and
Dohnanyi) through the Gestapo. You can imagine that we old
folks were quite hit by these happenings. All those years people
were under the terrible pressure of worrying over those arrested,
and over those not yet arrested but in danger. Since we all agreed
about the necessity of acting and since my sons were fully aware
of what they faced in case the plot did not succeed, and had
settled their accounts with life, we are sad, but at the same time
proud of their straight line of action. We have beautiful souvenirs
from the two sons from prison—from Dietrich poems and from
Klaus letters of farewell to us and to his children, that stir us
and their friends very much.

Finally, there was the letter from Karl Friedrich Bonhoeffer
to his children in Friedrichsbrunn, in the Harz Mountains, a
portion of which read:

For My Children

I would like to tell you about my parents' home, about your
grandfather and your grandmother, whom you know so little,

about my sisters and brothers, with whom I was brought up, about their lives and their destinies, about Berlin, the big busy town in which I met your mother. I would like to tell you about all this. Why? Because my thoughts are there, there in the ruins, and from where no news penetrates to us; it is there that I visited your Uncle Klaus in prison three months ago; he was sentenced to death. The prisons of Berlin! I know about them, but how different they are to me now! . . . I have accompanied Aunt Ursel and Christel, Aunt Emmi and Maria, who went there daily to take some little things. Often they went in vain and were laughed at by the officers; occasionally, however, they met a kind porter, who was human and who forwarded a word of greeting, who accepted something outside the established hours, or who delivered food to the prisoners despite orders to the contrary. Yes, to take food to the prisoners! It was not very easy during the recent years, and especially Aunt Ursel gave more than her share. She lost weight until she looked like a skeleton. . . . The last time I was in Berlin was at the end of March. I had to go back there shortly before Grandfather's seventy-seventh birthday. Uncle Klaus and Rudiger were still alive; Uncle Hans sent a message through a doctor, which was not completely hopeless; and from Uncle Dietrich there was not a word—he had been sent somewhere by the S.S. It was on April 8th, shortly before I came to see you in Friedrichsbrunn, that I telephoned the last time with the grandparents. At that time nothing had changed. It is more than two months now. What else happened before the conquest of Berlin by the Russians? A man who came from there told me that four thousand political prisoners had been murdered. And what may have happened during the conquest and afterward? Are all still alive? I wonder whether the grandparents stood up to these difficult days? Both of them had very few reserves. Grandmother suffered very often from fits which were due to too much work, not enough food, and worry. They do not have help in their house. Uncle Dietrich had talked to somebody on 5 April—it was near Passau. From there he had been taken into the concentration camp at Flossenburg, near Weiden. Why has he not been back? If I have to sit every evening alone in my room, without Mother and you, without being able to write to the Berliners [the Bonhoeffer parents and sisters] or to a friend, without a visit from somebody—it is so empty here and all my friends are dispersed—I cannot always "work." My thoughts are with Mother and all of you. . . . And when I don't think of you and am thinking of the grandparents and your aunts and uncles, I cannot forget what has happened to them. Therefore I thought I would write down what I wanted you to know about them so that you can understand how it all happened. It . . .

In reply to Pastor Bethge's question about how to end his book, I said that I thought the letter of Karl Friedrich Bonhoeffer would serve his purpose.

As I took leave of Pastor Bethge—and, by extension, of the New Theologian—it struck me as appropriate that, Pastor Bethge having first made Bonhoeffer's acquaintance in Finkenwalde, I should later have made Pastor Bethge's acquaintance in another retreat, the ancient village of Rengsdorf bei Neuwied. It seemed to me marvellously appropriate, too, that the account of Bonhoeffer's remarkable life should conclude with a father speaking of his sons and one of those sons instructing *his* children and, thereby, the children of his children about one family's sufferings —and glories—and its minuscule but inspiring role in a specific sequence of what is called history. My own particular quest had, in a sense, ended in a political thicket—the bloodiest one in the forest. Yet, I felt, all that the New Theologian considered distinctive in the contemporary spirit, and his calling now, could be found in the Hebraic tradition of the Psalmist, in the pagan traditions of the Sophists and Stoics, and in such modern movements as the humanism of the Renaissance and the rationalism and deism of the Enlightenment. Not unique to our time was the treacherous Christian (thirty pieces of silver was enough to seduce Judas Iscariot) or the doubting Christian (Christ's own disciple Thomas comes immediately to mind) or the denying Christian (there is Peter's thrice-repeated rejection).

Nor was unique to our time the Christian with eccentric views (the Protestants, once heretics in the eyes of the Catholics, were now "separated brethren," and the instruments of the Inquisition and the documents of excommunication and heresy hunts were already museum exhibits) nor the Christian who was a doctrinal maverick (central doctrines like that of the Trinity have been a matter of controversy from the time of their teaching) nor the worldly Christian (the life of Cardinal Wolsey, not to mention the doings of some of the popes in lustier times, will testify to that) nor the Christian distrusting reason even as he reasoned (Aquinas in the end had no more use for his "Summa" than Barth now has, in a way, for his "Dogmatics") nor the Christian without a vocabulary for God (the mystical experience in Christianity is as old as the religion). Even the "New Pentecost," whether it was Protestants or Catholics who awaited it, might, when it came, only start up old confusions. Perhaps the New Theologian was retreating before the rush of disaffection all around him. But then some lines of Matthew Arnold, written in 1867, came back to me:

> The Sea of Faith
> Was once, too, at the full, and round earth's shore
> Lay like the folds of a bright girdle furled.

In that time for which Arnold longed, I reflected, how easy must have been the dialogue between the men who talked about God and the men who looked to those men for knowledge of God! But even when Arnold was writing, only the "melancholy, long, withdrawing roar" of the sea could be heard:

> . . . retreating, to the breath
> Of the night wind, down the vast edges drear
> And naked shingles of the world.

How much vaster and drearier had those strands since become; instead of dialogue, there were now only indistinct cries from the edges of the ungirdled world as the New Theologian set himself the old task of equating faith and theology with reason and secularism, and doing so without any sacrifice on either side— a task, in its way, no less tantalizing than squaring the circle. But it was a testimony to the continuing power of the message, I realized, that there should be modern Acts of the Apostles, and that these should have the power to illuminate what Arnold, long before the Somme and Auschwitz, called "a darkling plain . . . where ignorant armies clash by night," and that shores far bleaker than those of Arnold's poem should be heralded as the world-come-of-age. Perhaps the New Theologian might find courage by remembering how the Psalmist of the Old Testament at times gave himself over to doubt and despair ("Out of the depths have I cried unto thee, O Lord") and yet praised God no less devoutly. How ancient was the problem of the urge to praise God!

I thought of the Magi setting out on their search to find and praise the King, the God incarnate. Yeats wrote about them in 1913 in a voice that was more truly distinctive of the contemporary spirit, celebrating, as it did, the connection between the idea of the divine and human suffering (between God and that blood-drenched forest). Yeats looked up into the unfathomable blue of the sky and imagined that he saw there the stiff figures in procession, the Wise Men on their never-ending quest. The Magi of the poet's dramatic monologue, with their abstract expectations, stood frozen, pale, and unsatisfied:

> And all their eyes still fixed, hoping to find once more,
> Being by Calvary's turbulence unsatisfied,
> The uncontrollable mystery on the bestial floor.

INDEX

"The New Theologian" was originally printed in serial form, and this is its second appearance. In the interval between the two publications, I heard from most of the theologians I wrote about. A few of them had suggestions for emending or amplifying the text in order to represent them and their views more accurately. I did my best to adopt their constructive suggestions, because theology, by the very nature of its concerns, is at once a delicate and explosive subject.

V.M.

New York
July, 1966